CYRIL DAVEY

Take This Child—
The SANTI Story

With appreciation.

Thanuj Vaac
July 31, 1974

Luisa

Lakeland

LAKELAND
116 BAKER STREET
LONDON W1M 2BB

Copyright © Cyril Davey 1966

First Published in 1966 by The Epworth Press

First paperback edition 1973

ISBN 0 551 00496 7

All rights reserved. No part of this publication may be reproduced, stored in a retrieval system, or transmitted in any form or by any means, electronic, mechanical, photocopying, recording or otherwise, without the prior permission of the Copyright owner.

Cover photograph courtesy of Fred Dole

REPRODUCED PHOTOLITHO IN GREAT BRITAIN BY
J. W. ARROWSMITH LTD., BRISTOL

Contents

1.	Riccardo Reaches Venice	1
2.	Tea for Two More	13
3.	Casa Materna	24
4.	The Prince's Villa	36
5.	The Violinist: Emanuele	50
6.	Fabio Outfaces Mussolini	64
7.	War Comes to Calabria	80
8.	'The Protestant Doctor': Teofilo	90
9.	The Lawyer: Fabio	101
10.	Death on the Road to Rome	114
11.	Emanuele Comes Home	129
12.	Casa Materna Today	141
13.	The Camp and the Caves	157
14.	'Casa Mia'	171
15.	Operation Ecumene	186

I

Riccardo Reaches Venice

'LISTEN!'

My wife's sharp command jabbed me awake and I looked sleepily at my watch. Seven o'clock, and I wondered grumpily why I had been so ruthlessly brought back from dreams to the sunlight of a September morning. Before I could complain, the reason was clear. From the bedroom next door came the sound of music. We lay quietly, listening to a master musician greeting a new day. So soft that it was at times almost inaudible, but suddenly breaking into excited chatter or an ecstatic burst of dancing notes, the music flowed from the strings of the violin, slipping from mood to mood, from brilliant cadenzas to dreamy rhythms.

Before we went to bed the previous night Emanuele had stopped at his bedroom door. 'You don't mind that I practise a little in the morning?'

'As long as it's not too early,' we had replied.

Now we wished he had wakened us earlier still.

When breakfast was ready I knocked at the door of the small bedroom, where our daughter Susan had chosen a tangerine wash for three walls and, appropriately, a wallpaper with Italian landscapes for the fourth. Emanuele Santi was still playing, looking out across the trees beyond Reigate to the green and chalk of Colley Hill and the Pilgrim's Way. Yet I felt his eyes were really fixed on the Bay of Naples, with Ischia and Capri half lost in the warm haze of this same September morning. In a thin, Mediterranean-blue suit, his stocky figure balanced in a musician's stance, he looked entirely 'continental'.

'I think I have not disturbed you? I remembered to play very quietly.'

He laid the old, fragile violin on the bed, with the bow beside it. It seemed a tiny instrument to produce such music, and yet it had been touching men to gaiety and tears for two hundred and fifty years, for it had been made by Stradivarius himself. When still little more than a youth, Emanuele had scraped his savings together to buy it, for he had intended then to devote his life to music. Now he finds it almost an embarrassment that he should own such a treasure when so many of the people he loves in Naples and the Calabria own so little. No one who knows what he has given in service to the Church and the children, or has been entranced by his playing, could ever grudge it to him.

Over breakfast we talked, as we had done throughout the whole week-end, about the children of Casa Materna... about his brother, Teofilo the doctor; about Fabio, the lawyer-politician who changed the face of Portici and died so tragically; about the war, when the children found such a marvellous refuge, and the years before the war, when Fabio faced Mussolini in the High Court of Rome; most of all about Riccardo, 'Papa Santi', with whom it all began—this magnificent saga of service to unwanted children, which has now extended so far beyond the walls of the Prince's villa on the shores of the Bay of Naples.

It was the last morning he was to stay with us and I asked for some 'printed matter' about 'Papa' and his work.

'There is not too much of it. No one has ever written the whole story. But it *should* be done. Papa was a wonderful man. The world should know his story. And Teofilo, everybody in Naples knows Teofilo. I have seen cars with licence plates from Milan and Venice outside his surgery at Casa Materna. And Fabio....' His voice saddened and he shook his big head. 'He would have been in the Italian Parliament now. Yes. It is a story to be written, and it should be done soon, before those who knew Papa forget what he said and did. But who is to write it?'

Suddenly he turned, cornflakes poised on the spoon half-way from his plate. '*You!* You should do it! *Si, si!*' In typical Santi fashion the dream of a moment had become reality in his mind. 'You will come and stay with us... three months... six months... talk to all our lovely children. In the summer it is too hot, but in the spring....' His eyes gleamed at the memory. 'In the spring *e si bello!*'

As if to add some other inducement which would cap even the Neapolitan spring he began again. 'You can go to the Opera at

San Carlo, where I played in the orchestra ... and go to Vico Equenze to eat *pizza à metro* at da Gigino with Teofilo!' He threw up his hands in delight at the prospect he had himself created, without even waiting for a refusal.

'*E mervaglioso!* When will you come?'

* * * * *

Short, stocky, brown-skinned and dark-jowled, Dr Teofilo Santi stood on the platform at the Stazione Nazionale, his hands thrust deep into the pockets of the overcoat he wore against the coolness of the spring winds which blew across the Bay of Naples. He looked relaxed and content, as if he had all the time in the world to spare. Indeed, this ability to talk and dream without apparent need of hurry is one of the paradoxical characteristics of a man who is endlessly creating new projects. At the same time, it is his unhurried interest in those he meets which draws them with such enthusiasm into his plans and programmes. He greeted me with a smile of welcome and an arm round my shoulders, though he had to reach up to put it there, and a minute or so later we had nosed into the chaotic Neopolitan traffic. The tough little Fiat seemed to find the traffic-gaps instinctively, with no more than an occasional stab at the steering-wheel from the hand that waved above it, for Teofilo talked and gesticulated all the way to Portici.

I had landed at Rome airport in the darkness some twelve hours earlier, seen the dawn colour the sky above the broken marble of the Forum and wandered round St Peter's where the priests said the first Masses of the day in a basilica almost empty of tourists. Crowding all I could into six or seven hours in Rome I had still been edgy to get to the end of the journey. Now, in the later afternoon, I had reached it.

A guide-book to the Bay of Naples which speaks scornfully about the slums of Portici is out-of-date. The road which runs towards Herculaneum through Portici passes an endless line of shops, cafés, tenements and houses which have grown drab with the poverty and sun of a century, but they are no worse than those to be found in many other cities of Europe and America. The real slums of Naples lie nearer the centre of the city. And Portici, as I was to see, has a magnificent road, owing its very existence to the Santis, which has completely changed its character and brought to it suburban apartment-dwellers of a very different kind from the black-clothed scurrying women, prematurely aged, who bustle about the alleyways behind the main road.

About five miles from the city-centre, we turned out of the Corso Garibaldi in Portici through a portico large enough to admit a nineteenth-century gilded state carriage—as, indeed, it had very often done. The gateway, in the fashion of Italian princely homes, leads under a large house which flanks the road. A marble staircase led to the upper floors. As Teofilo sounded the raucous horn, his wife Livia came down the stairs to welcome us. More fluent in English than she believes herself to be, she greeted me gravely and immediately flooded her husband with an account of happenings since he had left earlier in the afternoon. A schoolteacher by profession, Livia Santi is mother to almost two hundred children. Still young, she is quiet, self-contained and beautiful, with an oval face, gentle eyes and a trim figure. Daniela, who ran down the staircase to join us, had a shy smile reminiscent of her mother. Her 'Good afternoon; how are you?' had the precision of a twelve-year-old who had been learning English for a year.

My room was one of a suite of eight or nine guest-rooms on the top floor, above the Santi's own quarters. All through the spring and summer they are occupied by visitors to Casa Materna. In the visitors' book addresses in Britain, Scandinavia, Switzerland, Germany, Italy were vastly outnumbered by American ones. Throughout its history Casa Materna has been linked with the United States rather than with Britain. My room was sparingly furnished—neither the Santi's home nor the children's quarters have any evidence of luxury—but its firm beds, wash-basin and marble floors are gratefully accepted by summer visitors whose first act is to close the shutters against the heat. I looked out on the panorama below. My eye was held by the brilliant blue sea beyond the great villa which is the centre of Casa Materna, 'the home filled with a mother's love'. The Bay of Naples stretched out, on the right, beyond the overcrowded city to the long hill of Posillipo, clustered and crowned by the villas and expensive apartment-houses of the wealthy. In the distance, at the end of a peninsula growing hazy in the evening sun, lay the long outline of the island of Ischia, its ragged peaks softened by the warm mists. In the other direction, to the south-west, the Sorrento peninsula thrust out into the Tyrrhenian Sea. The Isle of Capri lay dreamlike towards its tip. I leaned on the window sill, unaware of anything but the exquisite loveliness of the scene, until I heard children's voices down below. Two curly-headed seven-year-olds waved to me as if I were already a friend. I turned back into the room, exchanged my respectable travelling-suit for flannels and a yellow towelling-shirt which seemed better fitted to the colour of Italy and ran down the marble staircase into the courtyard.

Within the portico I stood and gazed round. Behind me the traffic rushed along the Corso Garibaldi, a road whose name paid tribute to Italy's liberator, the courageous adventurer who had defeated the King of Naples a century earlier and brought freedom to the Italian people. Those days of the *Risorgimento* had given a new liberty to Protestantism. Yet it is impossible to tell the story of Casa Materna, however objectively, without setting the quiet courage of Papa Santi against a background of intense Roman Catholic suspicion and hostility. Now the mood has changed. But if the change is due in later years to the Christian understanding and vision of two great Popes it is no less due in Portici to the Santi family themselves.

With my back to the house I looked ahead, down a long avenue of overhanging flowering trees. At the far end was a fountain and beyond it, over the railway line, the blue of the Bay and the sky. I moved forward into a courtyard, backed by the yellow stucco of the long house, where the Santi apartments were marked out by the green-painted shutters and the guest rooms above by brown ones. Fountains stood against the walls of the courtyard—a woman's head spouting water into a marble basin, a lion's head spewing it into a leaden tank of pink and red geraniums. A huge garage, which had once been a coach-house, led off from the courtyard.

I walked on through the avenue of trees. A marble Ceasar stood on guard outside a sometime stable and a boy in blue engineering overalls unconsciously copied his stance. From within came the sound of machines. Beyond the machine shop was a red farmhouse where a farmer with a straw hat was mixing pig-food under the arcade.

At the bottom of the avenue, as I stood by the little fountain, I saw that an electric railway line ran between the grounds of the house and the narrow strip of beach with its lava-black sand. A tunnel connected the grounds and the beach so that the children could reach the sea without difficulty in the summer. To the left, backed by a ruinous Roman arch in the next garden, was a two-storey building with children sitting on the steps. This was the medical block with beds for some thirty children, though there are seldom more than a dozen there and, as a rule, most of them are ambulant.

To the right, facing into the Bay, stands the old villa of the Prince of Monaco, now the home of Casa Materna, the only Protestant orphanage in the south of Italy. Extended since it came into the hands of the Santi family just after the First World War, it is still clearly recognisable for what it once was. The wide pillared verandah, the domed entrance hall, the great rooms (many of them now divided and turned into dormitories and bathrooms), the statues and paintings, the deep basements once used to prepare food for ducal banquets, the red stucco which matches that at Pompeii and Herculaneum . . . these mark it out as the eighteenth-century palace of a Bourbon prince.

The lovely grounds have other buildings, some of them bigger than the villa. A great block near by, partly shielded by plaited bamboo screens, houses the school. Another modern concrete building, its square, modern lines softened by palmtrees, is used as dormitories for older boys. Flanking it, the Prince's tiny private chapel has become part of a long, low building with carpentry, television and radio workshops. But it is to the old villa, extended at the sides and with an added storey in the centre, that the eye returns. Its warm red colour glows against the statues, busts and columns, excavated from Herculaneum, which gleam whitely amongst the bright green lawns and darker flower-littered bushes.

Along the canopy above the pillars white letters speak the message of Casa Materna.

Lasciate i fanciulli venire a me.

'Suffer the children to come unto me.'

They are the words of Jesus himself. Riccardo Santi took them as a literal command, and though he died in 1961 his spirit still seems to abide here.

I saw children everywhere I went. There were girls clustered on the roof of the villa, talking and sewing in the sunshine. There were children on the steps of the medical block; juniors playing football on the concrete beyond the villa, older boys at work in the machine-shop and the carpentry building. A blue bus, with *Casa Materna* painted on the side, was loading up with children outside the school. Daniela Santi was exchanging excited secrets with an orphan girl, her particular friend, who lived in the Santi house. Many of them wore blue smocks and overalls, apart from the kindergarten children who had white ones, for the Italian Government insists that protective clothing of these colours must be worn by all children at school. Indeed, blue is the colour I shall always associate with Casa Materna. The blue of the sky and the wide seascape. Blue-clad children. Blue buses. All seen against the green of the grounds and the deep fading red of the Prince's villa. It seemed to be a colour of joy, love and hope.

A group of girls playing some Italian form of round-game smiled gaily, broke the ring and tried to draw me in. Suddenly their action became a symbol of all that this wonderful Home had been doing for sixty years. With a smile of welcome it had taken the stranger, the frightened child, sometimes from the streets, sometimes from the wrecked villages which had stood in the path of an eruption or the centre of an earthquake, often from the beginnings of a life of petty crime or beggary, not seldom from parents who had no money and no work... had taken such children and drawn them in gently and lovingly until they also were part of the great family circle and were themselves eager to open their hands and draw others in, too.

This, indeed—though it contained much else that I knew nothing about as I stood with the gay, friendly children—was the Santi Story.

* * * * *

It might be said that the Santi Story begins with the birth of Riccardo Santi in 1871. More truly it began with an Englishwoman who had been on holiday in Venice that same summer. Belonging to what the Victorians called the 'leisured classes', with enough money to take a prolonged holiday and enough courage to spend the summer alone in Italy, she had chosen Venice as a centre in which to recuperate after a long illness and, at the same time, stimulate her mind with the culture so much admired by her generation.

But at heart she was more than a sightseer. She was touched with the same sense of compassion which made some women nurses and others missionaries in a day when both were daring professions. Beggars, many of them children, whined for money from a woman who, in her own country, would have expected to see even the youngest of them at work in some useful and honest occupation. 'Sweated labour' would not have horrified her, in 1871, as much as idleness did. The British colony in Venice had grown used to the sight of ragged children, whining the blessings of the saints on those who dropped a coin in their filthy hands. To her, the sight demanded action.

Then, unexpectedly, the doctor told her she was still not well enough to face the rigours of an English winter. She must stay where she was, in Venice, until the spring. The young gentlewoman no longer wasted time in staring at the marbles and gilt of the innumerable churches. Instead, she began to collect money from her friends and from everyone in the British colony to whom she was introduced. A Protestant building already existed in Venice, with an ex-priest who had become a minister of the Methodist Church in charge of it. This young man, Serafino Beruatto, who had broken away from his traditional faith soon after Garibaldi's revolution, had plenty of courage. He listened eagerly to the Englishwoman's suggestion that a Home might be founded for orphan boys where they could learn respectable trades and be fitted for a useful life. With her aid an Industrial School was begun in two rooms and Beruatto became its headmaster. Six years later a hostel was clearly seen to be needed for real discipline and effectiveness and a disused church was bought and reconstructed for the purpose. An ex-sergeant taught reading and writing. Beruatto was in charge of the Home's religious life. Shoe-making, cardboard box-making, carpentry, bookbinding took their places in a very practical curriculum and older boys were apprenticed out to tradesmen and craftsmen in the city.

Within a few years of its inception the Industrial Home was well-staffed and filled with poor boys only too ready to learn. It was the first Protestant orphanage in the whole of Italy and continued its existence until the Second World War. The Victorian gentlewoman who had holidayed in Venice had wrought better than she could have known.

* * * * *

At the foot of the Appenines lies the town of Bologna. Its walls, five or six miles in circumference, enclose one of the oldest and most notable towns of Northern Italy. Men lived on this site before the Romans built their homes, temples and theatres here. Dukes and princes lavished money on palaces and noble buildings, while the pious and those who wished to be remembered by posterity employed artists, sculptors and architects to build and ornament the city's profusion of churches. From a distance the gothic basilica of St Petronio, the archipiscopal cathedral, the church of St Domenico with the splendid tomb of Saint Dominic, the leaning tower of Garisenda, and the 320 foot tower, *degli Asinelli*, strange and slender, dominate the uneven roof-lines of the city.

Bologna, however, has more than churches and palaces to draw the tourist whose imagination can recreate the past. Its university has been famous for centuries. It claims that in its medical school the science of anatomy was first begun. Its law school was equally renowned. The names of its scholars include Dante, Petrarch, Tasso, Copernicus and Galvani.

To Buonafede Santi these names meant little and instinctively he rebelled against the demands made by the splendid churches and their priests and monks. By temperament he was a Protestant and a liberal, though he knew nothing of the political and religious world beyond Catholic Italy.

As an apprentice carpenter young Buonafede was sent to work in the home of an Englishman living in Bologna.

'Can you read?' the foreigner asked one day.

'Yes.' It was not every workman in Bologna who could have made the same answer.

'Have you read the Bible?'

Buonafede looked at his questioner, startled. 'Nobody but the priest can read the Bible. He does it at Mass, in Latin. I can only read Italian, not the languages of priests and scholars.'

'Would you like to read one—in your own tongue?'

It was a dangerous question to answer. 'No Catholic may have one in his possession. There would be trouble if he were found out.'

The Englishman pressed his point, for there was an eagerness in the young man's tentative refusal which belied his words. 'Would you read it if I gave you one?'

Buonafede nodded. 'I might. Yes. But I would have to hide it.'

Carpenter as he was, there was little difficulty in making a secret recess in his own chair at home. There, except when he read it in such lonely moments as he could find, it lay hidden until he was married.

A century ago Italy was a country of divided states and provinces, many of them under the domination of foreign powers. Austria was master of Lombardy and Venice. France controlled Rome and, under her vigilant eye, the Pope ruled the Vatican States. Francis II, with his palaces in Naples and his Bourbon princes in their villas along the shore towards Portici and Herculaneum, ruled over the Two Kingdoms, Naples and Sicily.

It is unnecessary to follow the events of the mid-century in detail. The dominant figures in the Italian drama of liberation were King Victor Emanuel II, Cavour his Prime Minister, the liberal, Giuseppe Garibaldi, exiled in America, and above all, Mazzini, the champion of freedom. Cavour was a supporter of the Soziete Nazionale, whose battlecry was 'Unity, Independence and Victor Emanuel'. Garibaldi, taking his example from the nations who had rebelled against their autocratic rulers in 1848, 'the year of revolutions', landed in Sicily, called for volunteers to whom he promised 'no food, no uniforms, forced marches and glory' and gathered a ragged army who were to be known to history as 'Garibaldi's Thousand'. With his freedom-fighters he drove through Sicily, crossed to the mainland, fought his way north to Naples and prepared to do battle with the Ruler of the Two Kingdoms. Francis II, supersitious, crude and frightened, fled before Garibaldi reached the city and the fiery patriot entered Naples as its conqueror and dictator.

At the same time insurrections were breaking out in the Papal States. Victor Emanuel rode into Naples, where Garibaldi was wise enough to hand his army over immediately to the king. Together with Cavour, he defeated the Papal States at Castelfiderno and the Neapolitans under Francis at the Volturno River

—a battlefield which was to have its own place in the Santi story of later times. In 1870 Italy became a united nation under Victor Emanuel. The Pope relinquished his temporal sovereignty over the Papal States and retired to the Vatican with a guarantee of extra-territorial status for his new limited dominion around St Peter's. A liberalism strange to Italy began to change the country's political life and, with significance for not a few rebellious minds, Evangelical religion was offered a new freedom. Protestantism was to remain for the greater part of a century, however, a timid and ingrown faith, after the first rebellious efflux of sceptical priests and laity in the first years of liberty.

So it came about that Bologna, instead of being one of the Papal States, became a province of United Italy. So, too, the three sons of Buonafede and Luigina Santi grew up in a Protestant home, for the carpenter and his wife were amongst the first to discard their token allegiance to the Roman Church.

The eldest boy, Tito, entered the service of the State Railways. The second, Giovanni, became a teacher and later a supervisor of secondary schools in Bologna. There was always to be a very practical interest in education amongst the Santis. But for the third son, Riccardo, there seemed little hope of his achieving anything at all. Buonafede Santi died when Riccardo was only five, leaving the burden of a hungry, growing family to his wife Luigina. Though he left no debts, he left no money either, and Luigina, ready to work as hard as any Italian widow must do in these circumstances, found it impossible to clothe and feed her children. An orphanage would have been the answer if the family had remained Catholic but, so far as Luigina knew, there was no help of this kind for the scattered Protestants of the new Italy.

It was at this point that the Englishwoman's compassion and the Italian widow's need touched each other in a way that was to have deep significance for thousands of homeless children in the years that followed.

The Industrial School had been founded in Venice the year Riccardo was born. But it remained a school for local boys. Not until 1877 was it transformed into a Home with a hostel for orphans from other parts of Italy. It was in that year that Luigina was most desperately in need of help. Two boys she could manage if only she could get help with the youngest. To her amazement a visiting Protestant pastor told her of the Industrial Home just being expanded in Venice.

But to Luigina Venice seemed far from Bologna and the railway fare for the hundred mile journey outrageous. If little Riccardo were to learn to stand on his own feet in the world he must go by himself. Someone at the other end would surely direct him to the Home.

So, one summer day in 1878, a small boy of seven stood with his mother waiting to take his first ride on a train. The engine, belching black smoke, rattled into the station at Bologna, its short, high carriages jangling behind. The wooden seats offered little comfort and the atmosphere in the narrow compartments was stifling with summer heat. Incoming passengers struggled up the high steps with typical Italian disregard of those who wanted to come out of the carriage first. Riccardo felt himself hoisted up from below, with no more time to listen to the good advice of his mother. His thin body was heaved into the mêlée by a strong peasant who had been visiting someone in the city. His little bundle of clothes, which he had lost as he climbed up, suddenly appeared through the open window. He clutched it tightly to his thin body, anxious not to lose this one link with his mother on the platform. Then, without time to shout more than a sob-choked farewell, he felt the carriage jolt.

'*Arrivederci, mamma mia!*'

His cry was lost in the noise of the engine and the crashing of the carriages. The sun-bleached houses began to speed past the windows. The town walls were behind them and the uneven skyline of domes and campaniles slipped quickly into the near distance. At last only the slim *degli Asinelli* tower pierced the blue sky from the flat land below.

Bologna, with the safety of the little house and the sound of his mother's voice, was gone. Riccardo Santi was on his way to Venice. The Santi story had really begun.

2

Tea for Two More

'I DON'T like bean soup!'

The thin boys at each side of the newcomer plunged their spoons into the bowls before them, and drew them out heaped with small, solid beans. Perhaps they really liked them or perhaps they were just hungry, thought little Riccardo, glaring angrily at his own full earthenware bowl. He was hungry, too—but not so hungry that he would eat this unappetising food. He looked up again and saw the headmaster staring at him, his dark face untouched by sympathy.

'Well?' demanded Beruatto.

'I won't eat bean soup!'

The answer was crisp. 'Then you can go outside.'

Riccardo, wishing he could run all the long miles home to Bologna, stumped from the room. It was his first meal in Venice and all the magic had been stolen from the day. The long, crowded train journey, followed by the excitement of riding along the canal . . . the bizarre splendour of the oriental cathedral of San Marco with the campanile beside it—not nearly as good as Bologna's *degli Asinelli*, thought Riccardo to himself . . . his first sight of the great lagoon in which Venice was built . . . these enthralling things became insignificant when his first meal was bean-soup—or nothing. He looked through the window and saw the boys eating plates of succulent meat. His slight body stiffened with new anger and his tongue touched his lips hungrily. He pushed the door and went back into the room.

'*Signore!*' He addressed the back of Pastor Beruatto, who did not turn round. 'I would like some meat, please.'

'Your soup is still there.'

'My mother would not make me eat it.'

The headmaster shrugged his shoulders indifferently. 'Your

mother doesn't have to feed a score of hungry boys. You don't have to eat it here, either. But', his dark eyes narrowed remorselessly, 'you'll get no meat until you do!'

Riccardo had a full share of his father's rebellious temperament. It was to run in the blood of all his own family in their turn. But you cannot defy the whole world when you are only seven or eight years old and your stomach gets emptier and emptier. Riccardo refused the pottage for two days and then capitulated. He was surprised but not deterred to find the meat rather tough.

Serafino Beruatto was stern. His own rigorous training for the priesthood left him with no wish to indulge boys who were always likely to find life hard. The sun which ripened the grapes on the sloping hills would turn the ground to dust or iron. In their villages these boys would be lucky, at times, even to get one meal of beans or *pasta* each day. In the big towns there might be less than that. Yet those who were really in need found compassion in him, for he loved these small boys and created a home for them in which they were more secure and better trained than they would mostly have been in their own homes. Alongside academic learning each boy was trained for a trade and so prepared to earn his own living in a world where competition was sharp and working hours long and hard.

The Home was one of the institutions run by the American (not the British) Methodist Church as part of its work in Italy. Of Riccardo, five years after his entrance to it, it reported ' . . . very high abilities . . . hopes to be a schoolmaster . . . very conscientious and well-conducted boy . . . sets a good example to the younger ones . . .'

He was apprenticed to the printer of a local newspaper in Venice and, in such time as he could find in the evenings, worked hard at Latin and Greek. They came more naturally to an Italian boy than to a British or American one! He did not in fact become a schoolmaster, though an interest in education was to be characteristic of his whole family in the years to come. Instead, he became aware of a call of God to the ministry and offered himself to the Methodist Church. After working until he was out of his teens as a printer, studying not only languages but the Bible, speaking in the Methodist Church in Venice and elsewhere whenever he had the chance, he was accepted for training with great confidence. He was exactly the sort of young man the Evangelical Churches of Italy were looking for—eager, tough, studious, a man of the people who would never be outraged by the poverty in which a pastor would have to live, and, above all, a truly dedicated Christian.

The American Methodist Church was, at this time, opening a new Theological School in Rome itself. Just past his twenty-first birthday, Riccardo Santi was amongst its first students. From his room on the fifth floor of 38 via Firenze he could look into the via Venti Settembre, with its important offices and ministries. The Evangelical Churches were poor. Their buildings were often only hired halls, and the Protestant pastor himself would be as poor as most of his people. There would be little communal strength, for the Evangelicals were mostly tiny scattered groups which had sprung up sporadically, widely scattered, during the previous thirty years of religious toleration. To anyone but a young man of tenacious courage and hope it was a discouraging prospect.

To walk round the city of Rome was to realise the immensity of the task ahead. Both the massive solidity of St Peter's and the fallen columns and broken pavements of the Forum showed how deep were the roots of the Italian people. More significantly, when he looked at the Mamertine Prison at one end of the Forum, where the early Christians were imprisoned—possibly St Peter and St Paul amongst them—or the Colosseum at the farther end where these same Christians were slaughtered by thousands, Riccardo had to face the fact that the Church had always conquered those who opposed it and outlived them.

It must be remembered that the liberating days of the *Risorgimento* and Garibaldi's *coup* were still only thirty years past. At the beginning of the twentieth century, Italy trudged only very slowly in the rear of much of Western Europe. The optimistic liberalism and scientific pronouncements current elsewhere were still political and religious heresy in sun-drenched Italy, largely mediaeval in theology, culture and living conditions. The days when a gracious and shrewd Pope would be honoured by the whole Catholic, Orthodox and Protestants worlds, and would speak with affection of 'our separated brethren', were so far in the future that they were inconceivable. To Riccardo Santi and his

Protestant friends all the evidence showed that the Roman Church wished only to subjugate the rebels and build them back into its own self.

The young students at 38 via Firenze had no doubts that their future would be harsh.

But one thing comforted Riccardo. He would not be alone. His regular visits home to Bologna to see his mother Luigina had assured him of that, at any rate.

The lovely church in Bologna had been given to the Protestants after the Liberation and was largely attended by the foreign community in the city. Riccardo always found Americans and Germans there when he attended it during holidays with his mother, in her sombre widow's clothes. But his eyes were neither on the foreigners nor his mother. He even found it difficult, at times, to keep his attention on the preacher. The girl playing the organ had more than her proper share of his devotion and filled his thoughts when he went back to Rome to continue his studies.

Ersilia Bragaglia was a young lady with considerable gifts and, as events proved, very great strength of character. Tall, dark-haired and brown-eyed, she had an uprightness of carriage that marked her out in a community where all too many women and girls walked as if they were drudges. More than once she caught Riccardo's glance and looked back quickly at her music.

It was not surprising that Ersilia played the organ as if she loved it. She had received the diploma of the Conservatorio at Bologna where she had studied music and was a concert pianist in the district. This passionate devotion to music, countered by a strongly practical attitude to life, was to have a formative effect on the Santi story, for the young pianist fell in love with the student from Rome as irrevocably as he fell in love with her.

They were married at Bologna in 1897 when he finished his college course.

* * * * *

That same year Riccardo's name appeared on the 'stations of ministers' of the American Methodist Church in Italy and he was posted to Bari. As in many smaller centres there was only a rented hall and in a town notable for its veneration of St Nicholas the evangelical group were faced with sharp opposition. Riccardo was not surprised and as a minority leader he might well have become a rigid sectarian, for the temptation of the 'excluded' is always to become 'exclusive'. A posting to Palermo two years later, however, brought a new element into his ministry.

Palermo is the most important seaport in Sicily. It is also one of the most deplorably crowded and poverty-stricken towns in Italy. The heat of the Mediterranean sun robbed its ill-fed inhabitants of the desire to work. Wine was cheaper than food. Begging was the easiest way of gaining money. It was from Palermo that the stream of emigrants poured out of Italy, year after year, in search of a fortune in the United States.

Riccardo never forgot that his main task was preaching the Gospel. As a result of his work a new Methodist church was built in the city, and it still remains in use. Faced with people in need, however, he discovered that service is often the most effective way of witness. He was always a simple man. His preaching was never couched in theological language, but was easy even for children to understand. He was gentle and generous—overgenerous, indeed, with his tiny monthly salary, as his wife knew only too well. Above all, he was a man of compassion. Though the boatloads of men and women leaving Italy for America made him long for better conditions of work and living in their own land, he had none of the fanaticism or long-term dreams of the reformer. Instead, he gave himself to helping those who surrounded him. Children, especially, seldom appealed to him without response, and even when he had nothing to give, the day was transformed for them because the *padre* smiled and fell into talk with them.

In the poorer quarters of a Catholic city a Protestant pastor was bound to become well-known if only because he was an unusual sight. Riccardo, before he left Palermo, was loved by hundreds who did not share his faith. His direct preaching drew crowds every Sunday. His reputation for charity—or for being taken in by a plausible tale—brought a regular stream of callers to his tiny house. If he were deceived by sobbing women or lies declaimed with Italian exuberance, he accepted the fact as an occupational hazard. His wife, after four or five years of marriage to a man who could hardly manage to say 'No', was less susceptible to sad stories of wives deserted or jobs which would materialise the following week. To Riccardo, it was enough that he was able to help.

After 1901 there was even less money to spare. Riccardo's elderly mother, Luigina, had been living with them since their marriage and now, on August 20, a daughter, Luisa, was born. Three years later, on March 21, 1904, their second child arrived, a son, Emanuele. By that time they had moved once more.

Riccardo was still a young man, only thirty-three years of age, but the American Methodist Church, under which he worked, saw in him qualities of leadership which distinguished him from most of the Italian ministers. Someone was needed for the work in Naples, the metropolis of Southern Italy and one of the greatest centres of the Catholic Church outside Rome itself. The choice was obvious. In 1903 Riccardo and Ersilia Santi left Palermo for Naples.

It was to be their home for the rest of their lives. Within a year, Riccardo was to find his heart touched again by the same sort of appeal he had so often heard in Palermo. But this time his response was to change the whole pattern of their lives.

* * * * *

Enrico Caruso, who grew up in Naples while Riccardo Santi was running the streets of Bologna, made his debut at San Carlo Opera House in the 1890s. He gained little applause from his fellow-Neapolitans and was dismissed by the critics in the morning papers with acid comments. As a result he vowed never again to sing in his home city and, though he became the most famous tenor of his time, he kept his word. Yet he could not keep Naples out of his songs. To those who listened it became a magical city of music, gaiety, sunshine and pleasure. Countless people who heard him sing *Santa Lucia* and *Marechiare* yearned to hear them sung by the Neapolitan boatmen themselves.

Romantic tourists who were lured to Naples were entranced by what they found. The panorama of the wide Bay, with the purple cone of Vesuvius near enough to make the volcano darkly threatening, was not likely to be surpassed in their travels. Moving from *piazza* to wide shopping street or arcade they were surrounded by the delightful foreignness of the architecture, the people and the language. The Teatro San Carlo, with its red plush and heavy gold, was magnificent. The *Castel* dominated the waterfront. The royal palaces were solid and splendid. Flowers were everywhere and palm trees, oleanders and azaleas added a tropical atmosphere. Even greater romance was provided by the new excavations at Pompeii and Herculaneum, both of them an easy carriage drive from Naples itself. Though the historic University, with its records and achievements dating back to mediaeval times, meant little to them, they recognised the city's cultural and musical heritage. All in all, to the visitor Naples was a city of historic interest, with wonderful churches, intriguing shops and a rich past.

There were others who were horrified by what they found. *Santa Lucia* and *Marechiare*, they discovered, were not merely songs, but places—fishing villages on the edge of the town itself. The picturesque fishermen lived in poverty that was almost indescribable. Children were barefooted and in rags. There were men who, because of their almost complete lack of clothing, dared not come up from the beaches to the roads above the shore. While the fishing villages were shocking, conditions in the town were far worse. Men and women slept under arches, on the steps of churches or simply on the streets, because they had no homes. It was not surprising that tourists were beseiged by beggars, many of them small children. Naples, for its size, was the most poverty-stricken city in Europe, and hardly anybody in Church or State seemed concerned about it. Few orphanages existed in Southern Italy. In general, sunshine and theology together produced a lassitude in which both Authority and sufferers accepted things as they were, if not without question at least without action.

This was the city to which Riccardo and Ersilia Santi, with their two-year-old daughter Luisa and Riccardo's mother, came to live and work in 1903.

Riccardo was no tourist. He had no wish to visit Roman remains. The semi-tropical climate held no strangeness for him and he had no time to sit and laze in the sun. In the main, the great squares and shopping-streets did not interest him. He had come to Naples to save men's souls and, like the poor man he was, he made his home amongst the poor he came to serve.

His church was a tiny one in the Piazza della Borsa and the family lived not far away. For seats there were benches. It had no pulpit and Riccardo preached and administered Holy Communion from a plain wooden table. To his church and his home the old familiar trek began once more—men, women and children looking for alms. Now, however, Ersilia determined to be more firm than she had been in Palermo. On a salary of 90 lire a month, with four people to keep and Emanuele on the way, there could be little to spare for casual help.

'But I can't preach about love unless we show people what love is,' urged Riccardo.

'You can't give away what you haven't got.'

Riccardo thought of the homeless under the arches and arcades. Almost any sort of shelter would be better than their present plight.

'We could open the church at night,' he suggested, 'and let those who have nowhere else to go sleep on the benches.'

So the simple little building in the Piazza della Borsa became home for the homeless, and Riccardo was encouraged to think of other people whom they could help. Those who appealed to him most naturally were the children, and here Ersilia was quick to see what would be most useful.

'They can't read, write, or add up; and even the tiny ones learn bad ways because nobody ever teaches them anything else.'

'But with Mamma and Luisa, and the new baby boy coming. . . .'

Ersilia laughed. 'You're very sure it's going to be a son,' she said, and then went on more seriously. 'I shall still have time to run a kindergarten.'

Riccardo had no doubt of it. Ersilia managed time as she managed her household; she was always master of it, never its servant. To the end of her life punctuality was one of her characteristics, and she filled every moment of each day without seeming to be pressed. If she said she could run a school, the school would be run, and with efficiency.

The tiny church became a centre of social service where love was preached on Sundays and seen in action during the week.

The months passed quickly, and as if to mark the passing of a year of his Neapolitan ministry the hot sunshine of June flooded the Bay and made the alleyways more malodorous still. A second year passed. June 12th was Riccardo Santi's birthday. That year, 1905, he was thirty-four years old. To many men of the Calabria it was more than half a lifetime and Riccardo determined to fill yet more fully the years that might be left to him. But today, at any rate, there would be a celebration.

'Tea is at half-past four.'

Little Luisa chattered happily. 'Cake for tea. For Papa's birthday.'

'Now you've spoiled our secret.' But Mamma did not look displeased as she lifted her baby daughter. 'There is meat, too. Don't be late.'

Riccardo went out to visit his people, marvelling at the way his wife made ends meet. Cake and cooked meat together was a rare treat in the poor streets of Naples. He was, indeed, so eager to be home that he came back too early. Mamma's strict sense of time was outraged. '*Much* too early!' she scolded him affectionately. 'Go out for a walk... see some more people. Tea won't be ready for another half an hour.'

Not far away was the Piazza Nicola Amore, a wide intersection of main streets, where the buildings formed a circle round a fountain in the middle of the cobbled road. As he walked round it two childish voices spoke.

'Buy some matches, *signore*. For the sake of Our Lady buy some matches.'

The archway where they stood is still there, though it now leads into a domed arcade and two prancing stone animals guard the entrance. Papa Santi looked down at the children. They were a boy and a girl, very young, and he noted that though their clothes were poor they were not in rags. Nor were their accents those of children already trained to whine for alms.

'What are your names?'

'I am Angelo. Angelo d'Ambrosio. I'm six.' He pushed his sister forward. 'This is Rosetta. She's only four.' He thrust out the little boxes of matches again. 'Buy some matches, for pity's sake, *signore* ... *padre*,' he corrected himself.

'Where do you live?'

Angelo d'Ambrosio shrugged with the familiar gesture of the homeless. 'We sleep with our mother. Under the arches of the Stazione Garibaldi. She will come and fetch us when it is dark.' He pointed vaguely with a tiny, grubby hand. 'She works over there, in a big house.'

'You have no father?'

Rosetta's eyes filled with tears. 'Papa died. Only a little while ago. So we live with Mamma by ourselves.'

At that moment, as Riccardo never doubted to the end of his long life, God spoke to him. He seemed to hear a voice as clear as those of the children by his side.

'These children belong to me. Take them and love them as you love me. Do for them what has been done for you when you were a child. I will bless you.'

Riccardo took their hands. 'You must come with me,' he said gently. 'It's my birthday and we're having a tea-party. You shall come and share it.'

Ersilia looked at him suspiciously as he came in, a child holding tightly to each hand. There was only just enough to go round and two more guests, however small, were unpopular. Ersilia's practical mind saw the cake and meat divided into very small pieces indeed. Nevertheless, they could hardly be turned out again if Papa had brought them home. Besides, they were looking at the food on the table as if they had not eaten for days. It was a birthday-party to be remembered, though they could have no idea in how many towns and countries the story of it would be told.

After tea Riccardo took his wife aside. He told her the story of what had happened at the archway. Ersilia looked sceptical. Would the good God ask them to care for two children when they had hardly enough money for their own family?

' "I will bless you". Those were the words. Think of them sleeping under the arches of the station on the hard ground in a night like this. Would you like to see Luisa doing that?'

'There are plenty of other children who'll be doing it!'

'But these are the two I found . . . who were given to me.'

'We have no room . . . no money. If the money had come first it would be easier to believe it was the voice of God you heard and not simply your own pity.'

'If the money had come before the children we would have had no need of faith.' Riccardo was not to be put off. 'We can keep them just for tonight. I will go and see the mother and tell her.'

'Don't you dare bring her back, too!'

Had the woman been willing he might well have done so. As it was, she confirmed the children's story but preferred to stay where she was. Her husband had died a week or two earlier. She herself had found daily work as a servant in a house near by, but there was no room for her or the children to sleep. Anyway, in June it was warm and dry in the open air. But, if the *signore* wished to keep them for the night.... She shrugged as the children had done. Such kindness was acceptable. In any case she did not know what would become of them. If they failed to sell their matches there was no money to buy them food. If the *padre* could add to his kindness and get them into an orphanage.... She left the sentence hanging in mid-air.

Riccardo reported what had happened and Ersilia, like the woman at the station, shrugged her shoulders. They must accept the inevitable. Whether it was the voice of God or not, the children were here and the girl was dropping to sleep already.

In baby Emanuele's bed there was room for the boy, and little Rosetta was laid down beside Luisa.

'For tonight only,' stressed Ersilia. 'Tomorrow....'

'Tomorrow,' broke in Riccardo, 'we will do something about it. Perhaps someone in the congregation....' He stopped as he thought of his own poor church members. 'If not, I will take them to an orphanage. Somewhere there must be room for them.'

But, as Riccardo was to find out very quickly, for Angelo and Rosetta, the little match-sellers, there was no room anywhere at all.

3

Casa Materna

'THERE'S bound to be room in Venice,' Papa declared confidently, signing the letter he had written to the orphanage in which he himself had grown up.

'I hope so!' Ersilia still sounded disapproving of Riccardo's wild generosity in bringing the two children back for tea and the night. 'And I hope they answer by return,' she added as he went out to post his appeal.

He could hardly believe it when the reply stated regretfully but firmly that the orphanage was already full and the waiting list closed.

'I'll try the Waldensians.'

But the orphanage in Florence was full, too.

'What now?' Riccardo's face was unusually gloomy. 'My little salary. . . .' He left the sentence unfinished.

His wife made no answer but Angelo was ready with a suggestion. 'We can go and sell some matches for you, *signore*. Like we did for Mamma!'

Even Ersilia smiled, and Riccardo picked the boy up on to his knee. 'We trust in God. He sent you to us and He will tell us what to do.' He turned to his wife. 'The trouble is there aren't enough Protestant orphanages in Italy.'

'Why a *Protestant* orphanage?' she asked. 'There are Catholic ones.'

Riccardo rose half-heartedly. 'Not many of them round here. But I could take the children to Pompeii this afternoon and see.'

'Where is their father?' asked the priest at Pompeii.

Angelo answered at once. 'He died. And Mamma lives under the arches at the Stazione Garibaldi!'

'Then I'm sorry we can't do anything. We are dedicated to the service of children whose fathers are in prison.'

Ersilia did not need to ask what had happened. The stoop of her young husband's shoulders told her what she wanted to know.

'I didn't like it, anyway,' announced Angelo. 'It's too far away from Naples, and it had big high walls.'

Rosetta sighed thoughtfully. 'Now we shall always live with Papa Santi, *si*?'

There really seemed no other answer to the problem. Perhaps in a little while the orphanage in Venice or Florence would write and offer them a home. . . . Meanwhile. . . . Riccardo seemed to hear the echo of the voice that had spoken to him when he first saw the two children in the Piazza Nicola Amore. '*Take them and love them as you love me. Do for them what has been done for you. I will bless you.*' He turned to look at Ersilia and saw that his wife's face had softened, too.

'You must tell the congregation what has happened,' she suggested. 'Possibly someone else has room. . . .' She did not look at the two children, but Riccardo knew that, like himself, she would feel she were betraying a trust if they were handed over to someone else.

Not surprisingly no one in their little congregation would consider adding two more children to their own families. But, before the Sunday was over, gifts began to arrive at the Santi home. A small table, a couple of upright chairs, some bedding, a little money. At the end of a week Riccardo felt embarrassed by his people's generosity. 'They can't afford to give us all this. The Lord *has* blessed us—out of our people's poverty. We have more than we have ever had before.'

'That doesn't mean you can go round looking for more children selling matches!'

But Ersilia's comment was not as forbidding as it sounded. She did not go about the city as much as her husband, on his endless round of pastoral visits in the squalid slums, but she, too, found herself looking and listening to the children. Thin; in tattered rags; eyes brightly sharp with fear and fever; dirty hands ready to snatch unguarded food or grovel in a heap of garbage: running uncontrolled about the streets as if they belonged to nobody at all; unprotected by parents and with no security of home or love . . . the children of the slums were the background to their lives during the day and invaded their conversation and their dreams at night.

Ersilia was not surprised when, one by one in the succeeding months, more unwanted children found their way into their home to join Angelo and Rosetta. Some came because Riccardo found them deserted on the streets. Others were brought by neighbours or church members. Nobody could easily tell which were their own children and which were not, for at church, in the house and at school, Luisa and Emanuele had no special treatment. They were simply part of the growing Santi family.

The disasters natural to the Calabria and Sicily added to the numbers which crowded the house.

In 1906 the Neapolitans looked uneasily at Mount Vesuvius. Above the dark purple cone of the mountain the thin trickle of smoke was thickening into a cloud and, at night, the sky was red like sunset. Then, with no more warning than these portents gave, the volcano rumbled, the ground shook and a new eruption poured out of the crater. To those who watched, it seemed as if the top of the mountain exploded. Molten rock and streams of lava began to pour down the dark slopes. At night the smoky pall became a glowing furnace. Villages were evacuated before they were destroyed. Homeless and workless, the already poor peasants prayed to the saints for succour.

Help came in many ways, and amongst the helpers was Riccardo Santi, in his dark, thin suit, with a big basket from which he distributed bread and other food from the churches in Naples. But, if he went to take help, he came back more laden then he went. Here and there children wailed for parents who had been killed or had run away without them. Riccardo brought some of them to the already crowded house near the church in the Piazza della Borsa.

At the same time an earthquake struck Reggio Calabria and once more Riccardo, full of good intentions, took help to the stricken families and brought their children home with him.

Horrified to hear that Messina in Sicily, which he knew so well, had been almost completely destroyed he set off for the crumbled ruined town. His wife rightly guessed that he would not return alone. The first Sicilian children came back to join those from Naples and the Calabria.

That they all got into the house is incredible. Where they slept is incomprehensible. Ersilia was as committed to the family of unwanted children as was her husband. Nor were the demands exhausted when they looked round the big family, ranging from babies to ten- and twelve-year-olds. Day by day there would be a knock on the door and a tentative voice would ask: 'Is anybody at home?' The noise within had already provided the answer.

'They always know when to call,' commented Riccardo, with a gentle smile.

Because the wanderers and the hungry folk *did* know when to call one or two spare places were usually laid at table for the not unexpected 'guests'. The children would shuffle closer together and Ersilia would dip her ladle into the bowl of thin soup. Riccardo would bring the wayfarer in with his inevitable comment. 'There's always enough for one more!' There was only enough because everyone had a little less of the simple meal. In the evening it was a slim diet indeed, usually no more than a slice of bread and an apple.

The household worked on the 'do-it-yourself' principle. Ersilia —'Mamma' to the whole family—did the cooking. The older children helped her in mending old clothes and remaking those which were handed over to them by their friends. Riccardo— 'Papa'—cut the boys' hair, as he did almost to the end of his life, and doctored the whole family. His cure for everything from spots and colds to an aching stomach was castor oil—a remedy acceptable and effective enough in a country largely unused to skilled medical care.

In 1909 the family of twenty really did overflow the rooms of the original house and moved to two apartments in a building in Largo Porta Nuova. There, with slightly more room to move until bigger space inevitably tempted Papa Santi to fill it up with more children, life continued much as it had done in the earlier house.

If there was a natural family freedom in the home there was also a discipline imposed partly by Mamma Santi's insistence on punctuality, frugality and carefulness, and partly by the fact that each child helped to rub the rougher edges off the others. 'Fitting in' was essential to 'belonging'. Alongside all this, however, was the gaiety natural in a large family and congenital to the children of Naples. In a city far too closely built-up for playgrounds or parks the children played happily round the gay flower-beds and marble statues of the public gardens on Sunday afternoons, or listened, with the avarice of the true Neapolitan for music, to the city band.

Music was always part of the Santi family life. Mamma, who as Ersilia Bragalia might have made a name for herself as a pianist, not only gave the children the beginning of a normal education but directed their natural love of music. Piano playing and singing were more delight than discipline to the family.

But music will not pay the rent, as many a better musician than Mamma Santi has found out.

Papa was still the minister of the Methodist Church in Naples, and most of his time had to be given to that work rather than to the children. His meagre salary was 90 lire a month. Out of this the rent had to be paid and the children supported with what additional help he could get from an increasing company of friends. American Methodism was sympathetic but so far not financially generous. There were times when the rent was not only unpaid but looked as if it would be unpayable. On one such occasion the owner of the apartments made his own position very clear, his voice raised in an Italian crescendo of argument and threat.

'It is a good work that you do, no doubt, *signore*, running an orphanage for these thieving children! But the time has come for my rent to be paid and you have not paid it!'

Papa tried to break in; to assure him that somehow the money would be found when the children were fed.

'Not when the children are fed,' shouted the landlord. 'Now! *Tomorrow!* If it is not paid you shall all be turned into the street!'

'But this good work we are doing . . .'

The landlord shouted his final words. 'Do your good work with your own money if you must! You are not going to do it with mine!'

Papa walked round the rooms. Beds—yes, they could do without beds. They could sleep on the floor. Chairs—they had no real need for chairs. He called his own family and the bigger boys, pointing to one thing after the other.

'After supper we will take them to the furniture dealer. He will perhaps give us enough money to pay the month's rent.'

But after supper there was something else to be shared. Each evening the whole family joined with Papa and Mamma in prayers, the children praying in simple phrases, talking to God, their Father, as easily as they talked to Papa himself. That evening they could not help telling God about the landlord and the furniture which would be sold. Suddenly, in the middle of their prayers, a voice came through the open doorway. The doors of the Santi household were never closed, for there was no knowing who might want to come in. This time the voice had a gutteral, foreign ring.

'Papa Santi ... *wo bist du*? Where are you, *padre*?'

In the passage stood a German, and Papa looked at him with surprise. He was no stranger, but Papa thought he had seen him for the last time. Like a number of other foreigners, the German worshipped from time to time in Papa's church. One Sunday, a few months previously, Papa had been preaching from one of his common themes, that God has no favourites.

'In the sight of God, the shoe-black in Naples and the Kaiser in Germany are of the same value,' he pressed home his point.

The German's face grew red with anger. He rose violently to his feet, stepped into the aisle, clicked his heels and stamped out. Papa, despite his distress, felt sure he could almost hear the spurs clinking on his boots!

Now, not having been to church since, the man stood in the passageway holding an envelope. 'I am sorry I behaved so badly.' He pushed the envelope into Papa's hand. He clicked his heels once more, less violently and more formally, and bowed. '*Guten abend*, Herr Santi.' A moment later he was clattering away down the staircase.

Papa turned back to the room where the children were still on their knees, and Mamma looked up as he entered. 'God has already heard our prayers,' he said, turning over the envelope. On it was written in a German script *Per pio pentimento*—'In pious repentance.' He slit it open and drew out some banknotes.

'God not only heard and answered, my children. He has sent far more than we need. You can sleep on your beds again tonight, *bambini*, after all. And for many weeks to come.'

The ex-officer had indeed repented. The currency notes which

Papa took from the envelope were sufficient to pay the rent for a whole year.

* * * * *

It was becoming clear that Riccardo and Ersilia Santi had begun something which they would never be able to give up. Without intending to do so they had turned their house into the only Protestant orphanage in Southern Italy. The first distinction between this and other institutions lay in the fact that it was a true 'home'—without a capital 'H'. For several years, Riccardo's own mother added the matriarchal touch so familiar in Italian family life. The Santi children themselves were indistinguishable from the rest. It was the most natural thing in the world that the pastor and his wife should be 'Papa' and 'Mamma' to them all. Whereas in Catholic orphanages, which were never co-educational, children were often trained for the 'religious life" the Santis knew their children must earn their living in a tough and competitive world. Their concern was to give them standards of morality and conduct which might be difficult to apply but which would help to turn them into sound citizens and, in some cases, into real leaders of the community.

After seven years of existence the family numbered thirty children and the new apartments were overcrowded once more. The American Methodist Church, now more ready to support the work, urged Riccardo to find somewhere bigger still. The congregations at the little church in the Piazza della Borsa were increasing, too, and included foreigners as well as Italians. In 1913, new premises were bought in the Via Cimbri, only a few hundred yards away from the Piazza Nicola Amore, where Angela and Rosetta had sold their matches. The building, a long, four-storeyed, rectangular block, was purchased by the Board of Missions and handed over for Riccardo Santi to develop his work in the way he thought best.

The ground floor was, in part, transformed into a chapel—a simple room with benches, a plain wooden table for the celebration of Holy Communion and a pulpit. Four flats were to be used by the Santis as their own apartments, and the rest rented out to provide income. Each of the flats had half a dozen rooms, most of them big enough to accommodate three or four beds. Yet within a year or so, despite its apparently ample accommodation, there were sixty or seventy children filling the rooms.

Now, however, Riccardo was no longer supported only by a few casual wellwishers. He established a Committee to whom he could turn for advice and help, and from somewhere—no one knows where—came the name by which the home was afterwards to be known—*Casa Materna*. The 'Casa Materna Committee' was largely non-Italian. There were businessmen from the British colony in Naples; a hotelier; the wife of a British businessman; some Swiss ladies; representatives of the American Methodist Church, though there was at that time no American colony in Naples. Its most influential member was Dario Ascarelli, an Italian Jew who was a member of the Naples Municipality. Yet, in spite of this growing support and interest, Riccardo Santi himself remained the true controller of all the work that was done. It grew almost imperceptibly but never grew out of hand. But, because Riccardo was a Protestant pastor, it remained the concern of a tiny fraction of the community. His name might be well-known in the city, Catholics as well as Protestants might send him children to care for, but inevitably he remained something of an alien. Fifty years ago the division between the two 'faiths' was the accepted and unchallenged way of life.

By this time the first two children who had helped to create Casa Materna had left home. Angelo d'Ambrosio, his love of music stimulated by Mamma's interest, had gone to Milan and joined Ricordi's—the famous publishers who produced the scores of the great operas. There, near La Scala Opera House, he worked at the task he loved—copying out and checking from their own original manuscripts the opera-scores of Verdi, Puccini, Rossini and the rest of Italy's splendid composers. He was to remain with Ricordi throughout his working life until at last he was free to fill his time with playing Bach, the composer Mamma had taught him to love best of all.

His sister Rosetta became a nurse in Rome and, later in life, nurse with a private family.

Many of those whom Papa had found in Pompeii, Messina and Reggio Calabria after the earthquake had left home, too, but the true Santi family had grown. Grandmamma Santi was dead, and Luisa was in her teens, and so was Emanuele. On February 22nd,

1909, Teofilo was born and two years later, on April 1st, 1911, the family was completed with Fabio, the third boy. Like all the 'orphanage' children they were brought up in comparative poverty, though because of the desperate need of many who lived round about them, it never occurred to them to rebel against it. Indeed, it bred a self-discipline which was based on Mamma's own.

'You've dropped a pin, Luisa. Pick it up. You never know when it may be needed.'

Pocket money was doled out lovingly—and its use firmly dictated. There were two tiny coins. 'One for the Church, Teofilo. Put it aside. With the other you may buy *dolci*.' Not many sweets could be bought with half of that meagre Saturday gift.

'Emanuele, you're not thinking what you're doing. Play that part again!' All of them were musicians, though Teofilo and Emanuele were the real masters of the piano. Mamma would permit no dodging the dull chore of scales. Discipline of mind and fingers was the path to perfection.

Outside one of the windows of the apartment house was a street lamp. Teofilo can point to the window today and think back easily enough to the nights when he and Fabio rested their books on the window sill when the small children were in bed and laboriously wrote their homework by the light of the street-lamp because there was not enough money to keep the house-lights burning.

The years passed. Children left to find work and boys left to join the Italian Army in the First World War. Naples, in that Great War so soon to be eclipsed in violence by a Second, was not in the front line, though the Santis felt the tragedy of it when two of their boys were killed in action. The war, nevertheless, added to the burdens of the home not only by raising prices and making necessary commodities even scarcer but by adding to the number of children needing help. Not infrequently soldiers brought their children, pleading that they might be accepted and cared for.

It was the year after the war finished that a great excitement swept the household.

Papa, who always shared his problems and his news with his children before they had their evening prayers, took a letter from his pocket.

'I am going away for a while. But you won't be able to guess where.'

'Rome.' 'Palermo.' 'Venice.' The guesses came tumbling out.
'Much further than that!'
'Switzerland.' It was as far away as the children could imagine.
Papa laughed delightedly. 'Much further still. I am going to the United States.' His smile was rubbed away by the consternation on their faces. 'I shall come back, though. As soon as I can.' He touched Mamma's hand. However soon he came back it would seem a long time to be away from his beloved Ersilia after twenty years of marriage, of working, planning, dreaming and scheming together for the children they both loved so much.

'Why are you going?' The excitement was breaking out once more.
'Will you see my uncle? My brother?' To Italians, especially the poor, the United States was El Dorado, the Promised Land where money could be had almost for the asking and everyone's dreams came true. Until about that time there had been little quota restriction on the entry of Italians into America and they had streamed out of Italy and into the United States by thousands every year. So many had gone that to many people it seemed there must be more Italians than Americans across the Atlantic.

Pastor Santi explained that he was to be the representative of the Italian Methodist Church at the General Conference of American Methodism at Columbus, Ohio, but it was enough for the scores of children who clamoured round him that he might see someone they knew, and that he would tell their friends in America all about them. When they watched the big liner which carried their beloved Papa steam out of the Port of Naples and across the Bay they went on waving until it was no more than a distant splodge of grey on the horizon, and then they went back to the Via Cimbri to cry because they might never see him again.

Before Papa arrived back in Naples newspapers came by post. If the language was unintelligible to the children the pictures were clear. There, smiling at them out of American newspapers, was Papa Santi himself. The children laughed and shouted at the tops of their voices, urging Luisa and Emanuele to try and tell them what was written beside the picture. *Casa Materna*—that was the same in Italian and English. Papa had been telling the Americans about his huge family in Naples.

'Will he bring us presents back from the United States?' the smaller ones shrilled.

'Silly!' the older ones rebuked them. 'How can Papa bring presents for *eighty* children? There wouldn't be enough room in his baggage even if he had enough money!'

Papa brought something better than presents for the children. He brought money collected from new friends in America for the work of Casa Materna. More important, he had news to share with Mamma and the older members of the family.

'I talked to the Conference about our work. And spoke in churches about it, too. They were interested; more interested than I thought they would be. They are going to send a Commission from the Conference to see what they can do to help us.'

When the Commission arrived, later in the year, they found that all Riccardo Santi had told them was true, and more besides. There was a flourishing school, presided over by Mamma, in the house itself. Luisa, now eighteen, was one of the teachers. They found eighty children, over-running the apartments but astonishingly gay and happy. While they were in the house parents came to the door asking admission for their children, and they saw the gentleness in Papa's eyes as he talked to them. Casa Materna was a venture that clearly demanded all the help they could give. In quiet corners, comparing the security and joy of the children with that squalor and despair in which so many children of the streets had to exist, they consulted and planned. Back at Casa Materna, in the apartments above the simple chapel, they sat down with Papa to talk matters out.

'We're here to help you. How much money do you want?'

To Papa it seemed that he could ask for the earth, so generous-looking were these American friends. His answer surprised himself almost as much as it shocked them. 'I don't want any money.'

'You're the first Neapolitan I've met who didn't want U.S. dollars.' The leader of the group stared at Riccardo shrewdly. 'What *do* you want, Pastor Santi?'

Papa's gentle voice was firm. He was putting the dream of years into words. 'I want a house big enough to carry on my work. A house with larger rooms where we can run a proper school . . . take still more children. A place where there is room for all the children who come, and good air to breathe. It is too much to hope that there should be a garden, or that it should be near the sea.' He paused, but if his voice had stopped it was clear that his

mind was still at work. His eyes looked far away. For the moment
he did not see the men who exchanged cautious glances with each
other. He only saw the kind of home he dreamed of for his children.

'Pastor Santi!'

He was brought sharply back by the crisp American voice.

'You shall have your house.'

Papa wanted to run out of the room and tell Mamma straight
away that their dreams were coming true. He wanted to gather
the children together and offer them more room, air to breathe,
a garden to play in, the wide blue sea of the Bay. It was as well
he did not do so. The Americans went away again, leaving the
Santi family and Casa Materna where they had found them, in
the apartment house where the singing of the children drew
passers-by into the little chapel on the ground floor, at the corner
of the Via Cimbre and the Via Duomo.

4

The Prince's Villa

'REALLY, you must be mad, Riccardo.' The members of Papa Santi's committee shook their heads in despair at his folly. 'You've lost any chance of a new house—and lost the money too!'

Papa smiled in gentle reproof at their distrust. 'They said they would come back.... They just want to be sure, that's all.' His supporters—Mrs Rae, the Swiss ladies, Ascarelli the Jew—were sure it would have been wiser to hold firmly on to the bird in hand instead of gazing hopefully into the American bushes. Yet it was hard to contend against faith, and they knew that if he had not had an unassailable faith in man as well as God he would never have gathered eighty children, unwanted by everyone else, into his own overcrowded home.

His faith was justified a year later when a letter arrived from the United States. A second Commission would be visiting Naples during 1919. 'And they want me to look round at any houses that seem possible. I am to show them what I have found when they arrive,' he explained.

The Commission's reaction to Papa's discoveries was disappointing. Nothing seemed to be right. Riccardo Santi, pastor of the common people, knew the streets behind the great *piazzas*, beyond the big houses and hotels that fringed the bay. It was the sort of place he was at home in, and it did not occur to him to search further. The Commission sniffed the stale smells of the narrow roads and turned despairingly to Papa.

'Are these the best you can show us?' Their criticisms were pointed and practical. Too close to the street, too far from the sea, not big enough, not near enough to the public gardens, not sufficient room for a school for the smaller children. One by one the properties were dismissed.

It was then that a man who remains anonymous in the history

THE PRINCE'S VILLA

of Casa Materna but who was to provide the real turning point in its development broke into the conversation. No Italian can listen to a discussion without wanting to have a share in it, and now the taxi driver offered a suggestion.

'Why don't we go out to Portici? I saw a good villa out there a few days ago—a big one by the sea.'

'What was it like?'

The man shrugged off any detailed questions. 'You couldn't see it properly from the road. Fifteen minutes, *signori*, that's all. *Si?*' He was already holding open the door of his vehicle and a moment or so later they were rattling past the docks, and on through a maze of narrow cobbled streets.

'Where is Portici? What sort of place is it? What kind of people live there?'

Riccardo, still half-dazed, answered the Americans in a small voice. On the map Portici could be found just beyond Naples itself, the last suburb on the road that led to the Sorrento peninsula. On old maps, however, the five or six miles between the two towns were dotted with pictures of green trees. Portici had then been the nearest true countryside to the city. Indeed, it was at Portici that the King of Naples had had his country palace. It still exists, with its pillared façades, as the Faculty of Agriculture of the University of Naples. Between the palace and the sea were the ruins of Herculaneum, where sporadic eighteenth-century exploration had revealed the old sea-resort of the patrician Romans buried in Vesuvius's most terrible eruption. In the woods that fringed the bay the Bourbon nobility had built their own country villas and amongst the most important was that of a Prince of Monaco. When the villa was a century old its owner offered land between it and the sea for a railway which would link the king's country palace with Naples itself, and the Neapolitans claim that this line, opened about 1837, was the first railway on the continent of Europe.

A hundred years later, in the 1920s, the King of Naples had long been dethroned in Garibaldi's revolution. The woodlands had been replaced by a clutter of houses. The aristocracy retained little interest in a suburb that had forgotten its rustic past and had almost become a series of slums. Though the villas remained most of them had been sold and were deteriorating into squalid apartments.

Now the Prince of Monaco, too, had put his villa up for sale.

The taxi slowed down and the driver gestured widely to a long, three-storeyed building backing onto the road, with an archway leading through it into the grounds beyond. '*Ecco, signori!* Behold the palace of the Prince of Monaco!'

The Americans looked without enthusiasm. The high façade along the street was sun-bleached, and a tatty board announced the agents from whom enquiries should be made, while heavy, long-unpainted gates closed the entrance. In response to the driver's insistent horn-blowing and shouting they were edged slowly open by an old concierge. The taxi jerked forward into the courtyard beyond. Papa and the Americans climbed out slowly, staring round them. They were in another world. Behind them was Portici of the grim 1920s. Before them stretched the Portici of the nobility, the Portici of the past. Slowly they walked through the courtyard with its wall-fountains.

Not even Papa's faith was equal to such a strain as this. 'We must go back,' he urged. 'We could never come *here*!'

The visitors took no notice. Instead, they wandered round enchanted. Past the cage of eagles outside the ducal coach-house ... down the shady avenue of trees with their scented blossoms ... towards the little marble fountain made whiter still by the blue of the bay beyond ... back to the courtyard with the long high house above it ... down again amongst the lawns and trees with statues and marble filched from Herculaneum ... down at last to the old villa with its pillared portico, its solid aristocracy, its deep red stucco. The Americans measured, estimated and debated as they paced to and fro. Papa looked and listened, incredulous.

'It's got everything we want. Two big buildings with plenty of room. Seven acres of gardens; a farm; space for the children to play. And it's near the sea.' They turned to Papa. 'Will it suit you, Pastor Santi?'

Papa put his feet firmly on the earth. He had often asserted that faith would move mountains, but a prince's villa was more than faith had ever conjured up in his most secret dreams. It was too far removed from the world of the little church in the Via Cimbri to be within his grasp. 'We could *never* move out here. There would not be enough money to buy it. And anyway the Prince wouldn't sell to Protestants. He is a devout Catholic. The whole of Portici is Catholic.'

'We're here to buy the kind of place you need. And as for the Prince . . . you leave that to us!'

The Portici property was indeed bought, though the purchase took place through an intermediary. But Riccardo Santi was right. When the Bourbon prince found that the villa and its grounds were being made over to an Evangelical orphanage he offered twice the price they had paid to buy it back. It was a subtle indication of the attitude which was to face them when they moved in.

First appearances belied reality. The stucco on the villa was peeling. Walls were broken down. A great deal needed doing to the two empty houses to make them habitable before the children could be moved. The gardens ran wild when the Prince's gardener left. By Easter 1920, however, enough had been done to make the removal possible. Eighty children, all wildly excited though a little uneasy at leaving the familiar Via Cimbri, rushed from room to room, up and down the stairs, stacking beds, books, school equipment, pots, pans, crockery, clothes, personal possessions. No Italian moves house quietly, it would not do justice to the occasion; and not even Mamma could for long produce dignity or order on that Monday after Easter Day. The whole congregation was there to offer advice and 'assist', while an ever-growing crowd of vociferous neighbours added to the confusion. True, nineteen-year-old Luisa, her mother's aide in school and house, and Emanuele at sixteen were reliable helpers amongst the general chaos, though Emanuele was planning his own quite different way of reaching Portici. Teofilo, eleven, and Fabio, nine, were inextricably involved in the mêlée. It became a growing astonishment that Mamma and Papa, with the help of young Franco Cacciapuoti, a former boy of Casa Materna, were managing to sort everything and everybody out. At last, by tram-trolley and horse-wagonettes which held thirty children or great mounds of baggage and furniture, the caravan moved off. From the excitement of the huge family and the handclasps and farewell kisses lavished by dozens of bystanders on their beloved Pastor, they might have been setting out for another land.

Slowly the vehicles moved out of sight. The noisy, demonstrative crowd on the pavement dispersed. Franco Cacciapuoti went back into the apartment house which had been the home of Casa Materna for the past ten years. Incredibly, as he walked through room after room, it was completely silent. He picked up a little shoe, scuffed into a corner by running feet, and walked down the stairs holding it in his hand. There was no one to take it. Riccardo and Ersilia Santi, Luisa, Emanuele, Teofilo, Fabio, the eighty children who had lived in this house and worshipped in this plain but gracious chapel, had all gone. Scores of lives changed because, almost twenty years earlier, Riccardo Santi had listened compassionately to a little boy and girl selling matches. Twenty years ahead... 1941... what would have happened to Casa Materna by then, he wondered. Could the family survive its transition?

Franco Cacciapuoti opened the door of the chapel, went inside, and knelt to pray for them. It might have comforted him to know that he himself would be a Methodist minister in the years to come, but it was fortunate that the hazards of the years ahead were hidden from them all.

* * * * *

'We'll see you at the Villa Monaco!'

Emanuele Santi waved cheerfully as the wagons moved off. He and his friends knew a more exciting way of reaching Portici than a horse-bus. Salvatore, Emilio and Alfredo Cecere had already been at Casa Materna for some years and were studying for certification in seamanship. Their mother had died and their hard-working father was unable to maintain them. Emanuele was easily persuaded to join them in hiring a boat and crossing by sea to Portici, while Papa had agreed, with his mind on other things, that it would be good practice in inshore sailing.

Easter Monday, like many spring days in Naples, was lighted by thin sunshine and threatened by dull clouds beyond Capri. By mid-day the islands were already misty, their outlines half-hidden. Neither the noisy caravanserie making its way through the streets nor the four boys getting the boat ready took much notice of the familiar clouds, and the children had already arrived and were tearing round the grounds of the Villa Monaco by the time the Cecere brothers realised that something worse than rain was on the way. The dark clouds had white edges which signalled

THE PRINCE'S VILLA

a thunderstorm and the wind, already rocking the boat, was moist and cold. Danger was unavoidable if they sailed on but disaster was certain if they attempted to turn back.

By the time the rain-clouds broke, the sea was thrashing the little boat. Moments later they were soaked by rain and spray. It was impossible to distinguish the Villa Monaco, and the tiller flailed wildly as they beat onwards, in what they hoped was the right direction. Then, wiping the spray from their eyes they saw the whole of Casa Materna gathered in front of a large building and made towards it. The children were terrified and even Mamma's calm deserted her as she saw the boat swallowed and then tossed up again by the waves. It did not seem possible that it could survive.

In the end it was the sea itself, rather than the boys' seamanship, that brought it to the beach by the Villa. Bruised and helpless the youths were hardly aware of what they were doing. Then suddenly, with a heave that looked as if it were glad to be rid of its battered burden, a tremendous wave flung the boat against the rocks. Its timbers splintered. Two of the boys staggered from the wreck, a third tried to drag Emanuele out and up the shore. Badly hurt and only half-conscious he scarcely realised that at last he was safe.

There were no recriminations. Matters were too bad for that, and Neapolitans had been sailors for so many generations that they knew all too well how the sea could play false to its promises of calm. The boys were safe, that was all that mattered, though Mamma wondered if she could really have lived in their new home had Emanuele been drowned the first day they arrived.

Emanuele recovered quickly and the Cecere brothers pressed on with their careers. Perhaps it was because of the events on that Easter Monday that only one of them, Alfredo, finally held to the sea. He himself became a pilot of the Port of Naples. Of the other two, Salvatore later joined the Italian Army and Emilio emigrated to the United States where he eventually became a wealthy maker of costume jewellery.

The stress of that first day, however, was symptomatic of other storms that were to thrash round the little community after its removal.

The children, of course, could hardly believe that all this wealth of ground, greenery, sea and magnificence really belonged to the family. Peeling walls, ragged woodwork and broken statues were taken for granted. A good deal of furniture had been left in the two houses, together with pictures and statues, of which some were tawdry and others of value. One statue, at least, had been excavated in Pompeii. But with more space to live in, there were more rooms to be kept tidy. Vegetable-gardens and repairs meant that even the smallest were put to work. There could be no loungers or scroungers at Casa Materna. Over the years before the war such improvements as were made had to be achieved out of a very slim budget and almost entirely by self-help.

The real problems that faced Riccardo Santi, however, arose not from financial or domestic crises but from the mere fact of moving into Portici. In Naples, big and cosmopolitan, the Evangelicals were to some extent lost in the crowd. Portici, for centuries a small township, was completely Catholic. Off the tourist route, not so likely to be sought out by visiting and friendly American or Swiss visitors, both the Santi family and the children quickly began to feel its isolation.

'The Protestants have invaded Portici!' In a more liberally-minded world the horrid rumour loses some of its overtones of fear, but to a community brought up to believe that Protestants were agents of the Evil One the threat which the Santi family represented was very real. It seemed that someone must have put the 'evil eye' on the Prince of Monaco that he should have sold his property to them. The local people, encouraged by local priests, demonstrated outside the closed gates on the Corso Garibaldi. Passers-by crossed themselves when they spoke of Casa Materna or passed the house. Even the children were not completely safe when they went outside. A priest from Naples, Father Lombardi, leading a procession from the cathedral in the *piazza*, halted outside the gates and knelt in the roadway, to pray that the heretics might be removed from their midst. The patron saint of Portici, Sant' Ciro, who had once been a doctor, was beseiged with requests for aid. It was unthinkable in the early 1920s that the time would one day come when simple people in Portici would say that one of the Santi family was himself almost an incarnation of this same Sant' Ciro.

One of the main practical problems which faced Casa Materna was the lack of schooling. Throughout Italy a desire for learning, sustained by Government pressure that all children should have at least a primary education, was offset by the fact that many small towns had hardly any schools and most villages none at all. The Italian people, despite their emotional and demonstrative love of children, did little to provide education or training for them and practically nothing for those who were handicapped, lost or orphaned. This was the result of poverty rather than carelessness, though the Church itself must bear some of the responsibility. When the Santis moved into the Villa Monaco there were no other orphanages and only one school for primary children. Their arrival stimulated the Catholic township into building a new church immediately opposite the main gate of Casa Materna. More important it stirred the Municipality into a new interest in education, and both Church and town began to establish orphanages and homes for deserted and poor children. A devout lady, equally devoutly opposed to the Evangelicals, left 6 million lire to build an orphanage in competition with Casa Materna.

'We now have many more children in our orphanages than there are in yours,' announced a local priest to Fabio Santi, years later. 'Aren't you sorry you came here?'

Fabio smiled gaily, remembering that he himself was also directly responsible for providing educational facilities in the town. 'No. Of course not. Our business is to serve the children, not to divide them into Catholics and Protestants. But if I thought friendless children would be helped I would try and build a Protestant orphanage in every town in Italy!'

Nevertheless, since only one school existed in Portici when the Santis arrived, something had to be done. In Naples Mamma had maintained a kindergarten in her own home while the older children went to local schools. Now, it seemed, they must all be educated on their own premises. In the large room in the centre of the villa, with its great windows opening on to the Bay of Naples, and in the music room next to it, the Santi's own quarters were turned into a school. Its staff, at first, consisted of little more than Mamma and Luisa with occasional assistance from other friends and some of the older children who were pressed into service in the kindergarten classes.

Luisa herself, however, left almost at once.

It will be a convenience to summarise something of her story at this point.

Without the brilliance of either of her three brothers she inherited a good many of the Santi characteristics. It would have been difficult to grow up in such a home without developing a true interest in children, but while Papa's concern was to some extent limited to a practical compassion each of the four children developed deeper and more probing concerns. Educational method, child psychology, paediatry, an involvement in social studies and welfare services were the natural outcome of growing up with children in need and investigating their case-histories. Luisa had the true Santi interest in education, her mother's love of music and practicality and something of her father's simple faith. Like the rest of the family, she never outgrew the family, though, like Emanuele, she spent a great part of her life thousands of miles away in the United States.

She was the only one of the children not to be born in Naples, and even she spent all her childhood there, coming to the tiny apartment in the Piazza della Borsa when she was only two years old. She went to a girls' school in Naples, helped her mother as soon as she was old enough to do so and, from her earliest days, wanted to teach. She graduated and gained her teacher's certificate before the orphanage moved to Portici. To all Italians America seemed like Utopia and even those who did not want to settle there naturally turned to it for further education. In 1921 Luisa went to the United States, with some help from the American Methodist Church, to study at Columbia University. Specialising in psychology and child-guidance, she gained her M.A. and returned to Portici in 1924 to become responsible for the Casa Materna schools which were beginning to grow in numbers and general acceptance.

Three years later she married Francesco Zaccaro, a sea-captain, the son of a shipping-line owner in Brindisi. The Zaccari family were Waldensians, devout and simple in their faith. Francesco divided his time between administration and the sea. The family settled in Rome, though during her husband's absences Luisa spent a great deal of time at Portici, often in response to her mother's appeals for help in the school. She herself taught music as well as general subjects. As a consequence of these long visits to Portici and her occasional absences with her sea-going husband her family all grew up in the atmosphere of Casa Materna itself. Luisa had five children, all daughters—Marina, who spent two years at Bloomington Methodist University, Illinois; Clara, who did the same; Ersilia, named after Mamma Santi; Giovanna; and Luigina, who was called after Papa Santi's own mother.

Just before the Second World War Francesco Zaccaro went to the United States to represent his shipping line and settled in New York. Because of the war Luisa had to remain in Italy with her children, teaching at Casa Materna and helping Mamma to manage its difficult wartime life. She shared the allied bombing, the German threats, the astonishing evacuation and the return to the Villa Monaco. In 1949 she went to New York to rejoin her husband, though because of his shipping interests she was able to make frequent return trips to Italy to see her family and share the life of the school and orphanage.

Francesco Zaccaro died, after a terrible illness, in 1957, leaving behind a memory cherished by his friends and all who had worked with him. He was a man of complete honesty and deep integrity, whose faith lit up all he did. It was said that he could not go to sleep at night unless he had read his Bible, and those who worked in his shipping company knew that he would always be first at the office, in order to have a 'quiet time' in the place where he conducted his business before the bustle of the day began.

* * * * *

The growing work of Casa Materna, with Riccardo Santi's position at its head, might easily make one forget that he was still very much a minister of the Methodist Church in Italy. Indeed, he was one of its natural leaders. On leaving Naples he had handed over the Via Cimbri church to Pastor Nitti, whose family was to play some part in the Santi story, but he himself had been appointed Methodist minister in Portici. Even with no other Evangelicals in the town he had a considerable congregation in the children. The Prince of Monaco had a tiny but elegant chapel in the grounds of the villa, but a small altar and a dozen antique chairs were almost its only furniture and it was far too small to accommodate the children. Sunday Services and daily prayers were conducted in the villa itself but Riccardo soon began to plan the construction of a larger chapel somewhere else in the grounds. Reconstruction in the villa itself to make schoolrooms and dormitories was a prior demand, however, and it was not until 1925 that he began to transform the prince's stables into a lovely little place of worship.

On the ground floor of the long, three-storey house at the entrance, the stables flanked the road and were entered beside the main gateway. Riccardo turned them into a longish, rectangular room. The walls were painted a light beige colour with pillars grained to resemble marble in the traditional Italian fashion. The altar was moved from the prince's old chapel and served as the 'holy table' for Communion services. Ordinary seats were installed, but the old, carved chairs of the Monaco household are still in use at the back of the present chapel. A small gallery was erected at the back and a new entrance, in addition to that in the portico of the main block, was pierced through the chapel wall on to the main road. Above the pulpit, words of faith were painted in scrolls on the wall facing the congregation.

Predichiamo Gesu Cristo.

We preach Jesus Christ.

Che crede in lui ha vita eterna.

Whosoever believeth in me hath eternal life.

Here the children worshipped Sunday by Sunday, joined occasionally by visitors from Naples. In time other Evangelicals moved into Portici and new members were added to the regular congregation. Now and again parents and friends visiting the children would pause outside the main entrance, listen for a while and move on. Riccardo heard their passing footsteps and wondered how to attract them inside the heretical building, feeling it urgent that they should hear evangelical preaching for themselves rather than judge it only by inherited prejudice. One day he found the most simple solution possible. During worship the main entrance to the grounds was closed. Those who wanted to come in or go out had to walk through the back of the chapel. Now and again someone would stop and listen. Often no one remained at all. There were no dramatic conversions, nor were they expected, but to those who passed the simplicity of Protestant worship was fully exposed. There were no candles, no crucifix, no saints. The service was in Italian, not Latin. The preacher had no vestments, but his simplicity and compassion left the visitors impressed with his quiet dignity. By the time the simple ruse was given up some years later the need for it no longer existed.

In 1925 Emanuele left the family circle and emigrated temporarily to America. His story will be told in the next chapter but, like Luisa, he remained very much a member of the family, determined to do all he could to find support for Casa Materna's growing work wherever he went. By that time the number of children had increased to more than a hundred. The school was well-established and children from Portici were attending in small numbers as day-scholars. The chapel-in-the-stables was just coming into existence. Opposition still existed, strengthened now by Fascist intolerance, but one thing was now quite certain. Casa Materna was established. It would take more than opposition or criticism to shake its firm stability.

Children came from many quarters. A large number were from Naples and others from Portici itself. Casa Materna never had to advertise. Fathers whose wives had died, mothers whose husbands had deserted them and never come back, grandparents and neighbours with orphaned children on their hands all brought them to Papa Santi, pleading for his help. Papa never asked if they were Protestant or Catholic; he was there only to serve, and naturally the majority of earlier children were Catholics. Evangelical pastors throughout Southern Italy and Sicily wrote asking him to do what he could for children in desperate need. Sometimes they merely arrived, bringing children with them. At other times Papa went to investigate. When he did so he almost always found the conditions to be worse than they had been described.

'Her mother is irresponsible, her father's a drunkard. He leaves work at 4.0 in the afternoon, stays out drinking till the early hours of the morning, and beats the children when he gets home because he falls over them on the floor.' That was a fairly typical account.

'A horrid little shack,' said Papa on his return with two boys on another occasion. 'The ceiling was black with flies and they crawled over everything. The place stank because the animals lived in it as well as themselves. There were chickens on the floor and a pig in the corner. What could I do but bring them back with me?'

'I've had lots of daddies,' explained a small child of five brought by a kindly neighbour from the home of a poor prostitute. 'The one my mummy slept with last night was nice—he gave me *dolci* (sweets).'

Vice was not always a factor, though poverty was a constant. To those who watched the development of Casa Materna it was not surprising that the number of children grew year by year. The amazing thing was that out of such unlikely material Papa and Mamma Santi were able to develop young people of high character, integrity and rare ability.

Funds for the running of such an institution were not easily come by. It was hopeless to expect that orphans would be supported by grandparents or neighbours. Parents who cared nothing for the welfare of their children did nothing to pay for their maintenance. No grants were available from the State, though some Provinces did make small contributions towards the support of children from their own areas. Not a few past members of the Casa Materna 'family' sent occasional contributions or help in kind. The only foreign countries which provided any real support were Switzerland, which gave some little help, and the United States which, through the Methodist Board of Missions, was the major source of income.

The ten years after Emanuele's departure from home saw a gradual slackening of some of the local hostility, though it was maintained at an official level, and this was largely due to the growth of the Casa Materna schools. An increasing number of Portici children, almost all of them from Roman Catholic families who realised the value of the sort of education provided by the Santis, were sending their children each day to the school. Many of them, of course, paid fees for schooling. The number of teachers quickly increased as the numbers grew. By the middle of the 1930s there were between 150 and 200 day-children, apart from more than 100 Casa Materna children themselves.

In addition to his responsibility at the orphanage Papa continued his work as pastor and evangelist, preaching and travelling not only in the Naples area but far beyond it. From time to time he travelled yet further afield to gain help and support. He was fond of recalling the occasion when he went to Switzerland to plead the cause of his children. Doing his best to speak in French for the benefit of his audience, he tried to describe the work in which he was engaged, with its difficulties and results. When he finished the chairman of the meeting rose and bowed to him graciously.

'Pastor Santi, we have greatly enjoyed your visit. We are so sorry we could not completely understand your Italian, but the spirit of what you said came home to us!'

By the 1930s, however, new dangers were threatening the security of Casa Materna. Papa, though he took no part in politics, was an avowed Liberal, as were most of the Evangelicals. In 1919 the Fascist movement had begun to take shape and three years later Mussolini came to power. The little dictator, a declared atheist in his youth, who later gained the support of the Pope and the Roman Curia, was not merely to threaten the work of Riccardo Santi at Casa Materna but, before the decade was over, was almost to destroy its very existence.

5

The Violinist: Emanuele

FROM the very beginning music was part of Emanuele's life.

On Riccardo's famous birthday, when Angelo shared his bed, Emanuele was a little over a year old. He was born in Naples, the first of the three Santi boys, on 21st March, 1904. To baby Emanuele the d'Ambrosio children were his brother and sister, as were the other children who soon shared his bedroom and Luisa's in the Piazza della Borsa. The two sounds which ring in his memory from those days were of children's voices—and music. Often the two were blended. From the beginning the children sang hymns both morning and evening at prayer-time. In the kindergarten everyone joined in the familiar songs, demanding to go on when singing-time was over. Naples without the strumming of guitars or the sound of fishermen singing on the beaches or in the bars and cafés of Santa Lucia and Marechiare was unthinkable. The children did not have to be taught music; they brought it with them, one of their treasures however great their poverty.

Casa Materna, like Naples itself, was unthinkable without music. The early training of Ersilia Bragalia, who might well have become a distinguished pianist and chose, instead, to be the wife of an itinerant Methodist pastor, had its influence both in the home and in the lives and gifts of the Santi children. The piano was as essential a piece of furniture as beds or chairs, and even when it seemed that furniture must be sold to pay the rent there was no question of selling the piano. Little Emanuele started learning to play even before he began kindergarten at the age of four. Later, piano-practice always had to be done as well as homework, with Mamma's ear quick to detect false notes or poor rhythm and insist that it be done again and again until it was perfect.

At the age of six Mamma took him to his first concert—a quiet

THE VIOLINIST: EMANUELE

little dark-eyed boy, his feet dangled loosely over the edge of the seat, and Mamma noted the head and the small hands moving in time with the music. When a young lady came on to the stage and started playing the violin his legs and hands stopped moving and he sat forward, intent and entranced. He had entered Mamma's own world.

'I can sing that tune,' he announced on the way home through the hot streets.

'Which tune?'

'The one the lady played on the violin.' To prove it he started to sing, with a sharply-edged voice, the phrases he remembered.

'And he sang it correctly, too,' Mamma announced to her husband when she reached home. She was delighted. 'He will be a musician, Riccardo. He must learn the violin.'

'He is our eldest son ... our only son.' Papa looked troubled. 'I had hoped ... we prayed when he was born that God might use him.'

Ersilia, the realist, responded sharply. 'Can't God use a musician, Riccardo? I am a pianist, but I am a pastor's wife, too. Music is a way into these poor children's lives, into their hearts.' She put her hand on his arm as he tried to break in. 'You want him for the Church. But how do you know that God wants him to be a minister? Emanuele has music in him; you would have known that if you had seen him tonight.'

'He is already learning the piano; isn't that sufficient when he is only six?'

Mamma was firm. 'He must learn the violin.'

In a day or two matters had been arranged with the young lady from the concert. Lessons began—fingers on strings, the first untuneful screeches of the awkwardly-held bow. After each lesson there were sweets. Emanuele needed no encouragement though he was glad of the sweets. He practised with the devotion of one who was already beginning to find his true *metier*. Indeed, by the time he was ten he felt he had learned all the young lady could teach him.

When there was money to spare, he haunted San Carlo. When there was none he listened in the public gardens. One evening in 1914 he went with a fellow schoolboy to a concert at San Carlo, to listen to a concert. The pattern of his first concert was repeated, for though he now listened with a critical ear he was almost bewitched by the violinist. The red plush and gold ornamentation, the thought of the artistes who had begun their careers on this stage, the hushed audience meant nothing while the violinist played. The contrast between this man and his young teacher stunned him. It was not surprising. Giovanni Calveri, first violinist of the San Carlo Opera House, was also a professor of music at the Conservatorio of Naples.

'*Bravo! Bravo!*' Emanuele's boyish voice rang out lustily. '*Magnifico!*'

'Would you like to meet him?'

Emanuele imagined his school-friend was joking.

'We *do* know him—truly. I can introduce you to him, if you like.'

There was no doubt about the answer. One day after school, when Mamma imagined he was going to his music-teacher, Emanuele made his way, trembling with excitement, to the great man's apartment. There were a few questions, but not many; just enough to make sure the violinist's time was not being wasted. 'You're ten years old, you say? How long have you been learning the violin?'

'Four years.' Emanuele's voice was squeaky with something like panic.

Calveri nodded without enthusiasm. 'Let me hear you play.'

When the first few terrible moments were over the boy had no more fears. Indeed, he almost forgot the master who listened, unmoved, in the chair. Then Calveri held up his hand and it was over.

'*Ve bene*. That will do. You have promise, boy. You have music in your fingers. More important, you have music in your heart.' He rose, a dark man who moved quickly amongst the piles of manuscripts, music and books on the table and chairs. 'Would you like to be my pupil, Emanuele?'

He did not know how to answer. All he had dared hope for was encouragement. To be offered tuition by the leading violinist of Naples was beyond credence.

'It is impossible, *signore*. It would be wonderful ... but my family has no money!'

'Anyone can see you're poor. So were most of the great musicians of the world. But I never spoke of money, did I, boy?' He lunged forward, his hand moving to grasp Emanuele's shoulder. 'I believe you have talent, and that is enough for me. I will teach you all I know. For nothing, as long as you have nothing to pay with.'

Emanuele went home still wondering if it had really happened. More pertinently, he was wondering what he was going to say to his mother. In the end he said nothing at all, even when he went to his first lesson. He dared not tell Mamma that he had deserted her friend who had taught him for these past four years. One afternoon, however, it was clear that she knew.

'Where have you been loafing and lazing?' Mamma's voice cut sharply into his guilty soul. 'You have been missing your violin lessons! I met the *signora* and she says she has not seen you for weeks! Where have you been spending your time? Wandering around the beach and the ships again, I suppose?'

Emanuele found his voice—strangely tremulous, unlike his own voice at all. 'I *have* been having lessons, *Mamma mia*. Not with the *signora*, no. But from Giovanni Calveri!'

'The great Calveri!' Mamma stared at him as if he were mad— or, worse still, lying. 'It isn't possible!'

It took some little time to persuade her that it was true but, the explanation past and proved, Mamma was exuberant. So, indeed, was his little teacher. That one of her pupils should be accepted by Calveri was a distinction in itself.

The lessons continued and the years passed, though there was more to work at than music. Where musicians were as common as monks a man needed to do more than play the violin if he were to support a wife and family. Music must be backed up (no one could have been firmer about this than Mamma) by other professional qualifications. Like the other Santi children Emanuele won his way by scholarships, and passed from high school to the university. By 1922, when he was eighteen, he had already done his undergraduate studies in classics and had turned to mathematics. From that he went on to engineering. But the variety of his qualifications only showed how uncertain he was about his true vocation. Unlike Luisa, he did not take naturally to teaching —and his own wishes met with strong opposition, though he attended regularly at the Conservatorio where Giovanni Calveri was becoming as much friend as tutor.

'I was born to play the violin', explained Emanuele to his father.

'You think you can make your living from a fiddle?' demanded Papa with rare tartness. 'What an example to the rest of these children. We try to teach them to work hard—and you want to go and play the violin?' Papa's gentle face grew stubborn. 'I won't have it, Emanuele!'

At seventeen he gained a diploma from the Conservatorio; two years later he gained his second. Mamma was delighted, Papa proud but uneasy. Emanuele well understood the real point of tension. It was not that Papa objected to him becoming a musician, any more than he wanted him to be an engineer. Riccardo Santi had always longed that his eldest son should be a minister of the Church. But, to Emanuele, one parson in the family was enough. Besides, at sixteen Teofilo was already interested in the Church. And Fabio, though he seemed to think of nothing but sport, was a good mixer and never stopped talking. Perhaps, thought Emanuele, one of *them* would fulfil Papa's great ambition. He himself had already played in symphony concerts at San Carlo Opera House and knew he would be happier on a concert platform than in a pulpit. In any case, he argued, why should God have given him such talents unless He meant him to use them?

By the time Casa Materna had been established at Portici for three years Emanuele was finished with the university and had made up his mind to spend some time in Switzerland thinking and praying his way through the situation. There was another compelling reason for his leaving Italy. At the University he had joined an undergraduates' society, the *Corda Fratres*, which was pledged to Liberalism and to oppose the Fascist principles of Mussolini. By 1925, when Emanuele was twenty-one and due to leave the university, Mussolini was consolidating his power and looking for enemies everywhere, especially amongst the young Liberals of the universities. Emanuele had no mind to be hauled out of bed one quiet night by the *carbinieri* and dragged off to the police cells or to prison.

Naturally he took his violin to Switzerland, and a diploma from the Naples Conservatorio was sufficient to open the concert platform to him in Lausanne. There, he was heard with delight by Otto Barblan, the famous organist of the great Protestant cathedral of St Pierre in Geneva. Cultured, close-knit and critical, the society which really mattered in Geneva listened to his four concerts in St Pierre cathedral with cool appraisal. More significant, however, was the engagement that followed in the Victoria Hall, the largest in the city of Geneva. His press notices were encouraging and invitations followed from other towns and cities. He set out to tour the country. By the time he returned to Naples his decision was made and his future clear. He would commit his life to music. But how? And where? These practical questions could no longer be deferred.

Italy was becoming increasingly committed to the Fascist cause and Emanuele was already marked down as a revolutionary. Back from the United States, Luisa enlarged the descriptions she had given in her letters of life and freedom across the Atlantic. At this critical moment he saw an advertisement stating that the Conservatoire of Music at Newburgh, New York, was seeking a director of music. Without much hope that America would be prepared to consider an unknown young violinist from Naples he sent an application for the post and probably no one was more surprised than himself when he was engaged for the coming session.

Like Luisa, who had sailed from Naples three years previously to take her degree course, Emanuele stood at the rail of the boat, waving farewell to his family and the children. 'I'll be back when the winter's over,' he shouted into the growing space between ship and shore. He could see Mamma lift her handkerchief to her eyes and Papa waving. As the ship drew out into the bay the whole of Naples began to extend itself before him. In the distance, the red block that was the Villa Monaco became smaller and smaller. The liner stopped, and the pilot climbed down into his launch and bobbed away back over the waves.

Emanuele had cut the links that tied him to Italy, to Portici, to Casa Materna. At the age of twenty-one, he was on his way to freedom.

* * * * *

Entry into the United States was not as easy as Emanuele had imagined. Once there, those who wrote home to Italy were more concerned with the opportunities in their new land to describe the tedium and frustration which stood between the immigrant ship and the mainland. To the young musician Ellis Island was the place you stopped at before landing. He soon found it was more than this. Crowded already with would-be immigrants, the island not so far from the Statue of Liberty became almost a place of imprisonment. Quota restrictions were in force, and those who hoped to enter the land of hope were required to answer endless questions, submit to public interrogation and perhaps to wait for many months before the moment of entry arrived. For some it did not come at all.

Emanuele was more fortunate than many of his compatriots. The presiding judge noted his profession and made a suggestion. 'I see you're a violinist. It's pretty dull for these people here week after week. Why don't you give them a concert. We could find a pianist amongst them, surely.'

Soon afterwards the concert was arranged, and the hall was crowded with people of many nations. They listened entranced and demanded more—and more. Of greater importance, the judge too was delighted.

'You have a great gift, *signore*. We can use men of your gifts and spirit in America.' He looked Emanuele up and down. 'You intended to stay in America?'

'There's no place for me in Italy.'

'I will see that your application is expedited, Signor Santi.'

True to his word, the judge moved the application to the head of the list. Emanuele found himself, long before many of those who had been on Ellis Island for months, granted citizenship of the United States of America. He still remains an American citizen.

He did not return after the winter was over. His programme was too full even to return the following summer. Not until 1929 did he come back to Switzerland, and it was only in 1932 that he returned to Naples.

The first winter, as director of the Conservatoire at Newburgh, was not unsuccessful. Young, slim, with dark curling hair and thick glasses, he was a noticeable figure. In his publicity brochure the Stradivarius violin is held confidently between lowered face and lifted shoulder. But, at twenty-one, it takes luck as well as genius to conquer the musical world. Emanuele, more interested in music than fame, was content to set up as a teacher while he waited for the contracts to come in. At the end of his first year at Newburgh he moved into New York itself and opened a studio in the Steinway Building on 57th Street where all the great teachers worked. Many of those who could not afford the fees of the successful stopped the elevator at Emanuele Santi's floor and, because he was a good teacher, before long he had more students than he could deal with.

If music was his first love his other interests, education and the Church, served it well. Invitations to play in churches came week by week and he quickly found his way into the schools. He was devoted to children and, often to their teachers' astonishment, they listened enraptured as he opened to them the world of classical music. Within a year or so he was a public figure in New York, Pennsylvania and New Jersey. The 'blurbs' for his concerts explained his popularity.

'It is unusual for a school to enter so genuinely into a musical programme.' 'The most perfect I have heard in schools.' So wrote school authorities. In Europe more discerning cities had already given their own verdict. 'Very seldom has one the opportunity of hearing a violinist of such high interpretative talents', said the *Giornale d'Italia*. 'Power and dignity' stated the *Neue Zuricher Zeitung*. '... surpasses especially in the precision, purity and sonority of his tone ... he played most exquisitely', commented the *Lausanne Gazette*. More personal was a letter from Alonzo Diez, the organist of Lausanne. 'The day you played with me you gave me one of the most powerful and unforgettable musical emotions of my life ... I shall never again hear Old Italian music without judging other violinists by your playing of it.'

The one thing at which he did badly was English. He was so busy working that he had no time to learn. From 8.0 a.m. until after lunch he practised unremittingly. In the afternoon he was engaged with his students. In the evening he was almost always occupied with concert work. The two sentences he had managed to learn by heart, humble though they were, were quite inadequate to a concert violinist.

'Tank you ver' mooch. I will try to do better nex' time!'

Such Christian humility was not much help to a hard-working publicity agent! But as he toiled to master the new language as well as to perfect his technique the volume of bookings swelled.

With the engagements came welcome dollars. Emanuele, however, was genuinely indifferent to money. Indeed, now that he was so far away from Portici, he was more concerned with Casa Materna than he had ever been before. Many of his concerts were wholly given for its benefit and at the Villa Monaco more work became possible because of his musical successes.

Both music and Church brought him friends. He was invited to play his violin at one of the Methodist Conferences. Now and again opportunities came to talk at length about the work of Casa Materna, as well as to speak briefly of it during his concerts on its behalf. On one occasion he was asked to play at the home of Professor Harris, at Union Theological Seminary, and this was an acquaintance which was in time to have an important effect on his career.

In 1929 he returned to Europe, though he chose to meet his parents in Switzerland because of his anti-Fascist sympathies. 'It's all very well for Mussolini to say that it's better to live one day like a lion than a hundred years like a sheep', he explained. 'But I want to live my whole life, not one day—and I don't want to live it in a Fascist prison.'

Three years later, however, he did go back to Casa Materna, as 'Uncle Emanuele from America', to spend the whole summer with the children. There was no difficulty about the fare or about money to help Papa and Mamma in their work at Portici. His successful concerts and tours had put a good many dollars in his American bank. It was unnecessary to worry about a whole summer without working. He could afford to do nothing for a while. It was one of the joys of success. But, once back in Portici, some of the old tensions returned. He loved the children and found a sense of fulfilment in sharing in their games, the swimming, their music, their needs. He preached in the lovely little church, now becoming a centre of worship for others besides the Casa Materna family. The trouble was that there was no time for his own music. The gracious, centuries-old violin lay in its battered case, untouched for days at a time. His fingers flexed as he worked in the garden and he imagined the familiar shape nestling below his chin. He tried to keep his loss to himself, to hold back his growing frustration until at last desire would be controlled no longer.

'I must go back. I *must* have my music!'

THE VIOLINIST: EMANUELE

Not even Papa was really surprised, though he had longed for his son's continuing help at Casa Materna. Luisa was married and spending only irregular periods at Portici. Fabio was at university, and Teofilo was nearing the end of his medical training, after which he would have to do his two years in the Italian Army as a conscript. But for Emanuele 'life' was still 'music'. The summer over, he set off for Switzerland to rest and gain some renewed inspiration for his work, and to give recitals once more. With Alonso Diez, organist at Lausanne's Chapelle le Terreaux and professor of music, he agreed to make a five-week tour of the mountain towns and villages. It was highly successful, and the end came too quickly for both men. To continue, however, was impossible, for Diez was committed to lecture to a congress of theological and philosophical students at Vomazcus on Lake Neuchatel.

'But it's a pity to break up sooner than we need' he commented to Emanuele. 'I've written to ask if they would like a recital of violin and piano music at the opening session.' In the event Emanuele was not only invited to play but to stay for the conference. On paper the programme looked heavy and forbidding, beginning as it did with an opening address by Emil Brunner, one of the outstanding contemporary Swiss theologians. But it was this first address which did what Papa's loving appeals could never have achieved.

Brunner pursued the familiar line of Barthian theology. 'We are all nothingness in contrast to God's allness ... the little we have already belongs to God ... in no human achievement is there a place for pride.'

For the rest of the Vomazcus conference Emanuele's thoughts and emotions were at war. 'Am I proud? ... Is it wrong if I am? .... Practise has become no more than a routine, but concerts are different ... people are moved ... they see a new meaning in music and in life ... but am I proud? ... are concerts the whole of life?'

He salved his conscience momentarily by planning an American 'Casa Materna Society' but his turmoil of mind continued. By the time he sailed for the United States on the *Amsterdam* he knew he would have no rest until he came to a decision and held to it. He spoke to his agent and, Santi-fashion, there was something in his tone which implied that his words were final.

'I know what God wants, now. I am to become a minister.'

That the agent who arranged his concerts should rebel against the decision was not surprising. But that he should then be opposed within the Church left him more disturbed than before. He talked to his acquaintance Dr Harris, who introduced him to Dr Henry Sloane Coffin, the President of Union Theological Seminary.

The presidential 'Glad to meet you' was cool and formal. No word of welcome followed it, no encouragement met the hesitant story of his answer to Emil Brunner's challenge.

'You are almost thirty, Mr Santi. A bit late for starting a new course of study. And you're a musician.' It sounded as if Henry Coffin rated violinists lower than Riccardo had done. 'Keep on playing, Mr Santi. As a violinist you give people a great deal of pleasure.'

Emanuele had been speaking Italian and French throughout the summer and he could not shape his words into an intelligible argument. His fumbling phrases accentuated Coffin's word of dismissal.

'Another thing, Mr Santi. You have no command of English!'

Emanuele refused to accept the tepid interview as final. Convinced that he himself had heard God's call, whether Dr Coffin knew it or not, he enrolled as a student at Union. Financial support was simple; he had plenty of concerts and gave violin lessons. To most of the students he was a musician with an interest in theology rather than the other way round, but the three years at Union taught him more than theology. They gave him discipline, a constant check on his sense of vocation and a growing familiarity with spoken and written English, though he was never to lose his Italian accent or constructions. In his room near Henry van Dusen's he played his violin regularly and gained the sympathy and support of this Church leader—a fact of importance when he came to the end of his college course. He took his B.D. in 1935 and in that year was ordained in New York City.

Only then did he write and tell Papa what had happened. The reply surprised him.

'My Dear Son,
  I have known all along . . . I always prayed to God that you would become a minister of His Church. . . .'

For the next two years he continued his studies, and in 1937 he gained his S.T.M., and after working on studies of child development and education at Columbia University was granted his Doctorate of Education in 1939. By that time he had been in charge of a Methodist Church for a year.

In the twenty years he spent in pastoral work in the United States he had charge of only two churches, and his first 'call' somewhat off-set Henry Coffin's criticism that he had no command of English. It was to Yonkers, in New York State. This had once been a Dutch settlement, but by the 1930s it had gathered an international working-class population, with Poles, Finns, Irish and a high proportion of Italians. One of its main industries was the Otis Lift Company. The Methodist congregation was about forty per cent American and sixty per cent Italian, and his ministry had to be bi-lingual. Emanuele felt more 'at home' than he had done since he left Naples and his first 'welcome' assured him that he was nearer home than he had thought.

Amongst the Italian emigrants to the United States were some who had spent their childhood at Casa Materna. The first person to welcome Emanuele to Yonkers was one of them—Olga Ricci, whose mother had helped in the kitchens. Olga herself, now an insurance agent and running a travel bureau, was the Sunday School Superintendent at Yonkers.

He remained at Yonkers for fourteen years. Unmarried, as he still is, he was able to devote all his time to the four things he cared for most—the work of the local church, child study and education, the violin, and the Casa Materna Society. The Casa Materna Society, small but increasingly valuable, had been founded in fulfilment of his promise, when he returned from his summer visit to Portici in 1932. His concerts were the main source of its income, for there was still time to relax, as well as to delight others, with his violin.

In 1952 he received a 'call' to the Methodist Church at Castle Heights, on White Plains, New York. He was hesitant to accept. It meant leaving the familiar setting of Yonkers for a very different community. Could he serve a congregation which included highly-paid executives as well as he had the industrial workers at Yonkers? In the end he reluctantly agreed to go, and found the decision completely right. In five years the Sunday School and the Church budget doubled.

Any doubts as to whether the young violinist had the disciplined qualities which would make a good minister had long since been dispelled. He was loved, honoured and established. Italy was a long way off and so was Casa Materna. True, he had occasionally wondered if he ought not to return there, but the advice of his bishop had always been the same. 'You are an American citizen. You belong to the Methodist Church in America. You can do far more good for Casa Materna by staying here and pleading its cause amongst people who know and respect you than you can by becoming an additional member of a team at work in the orphanage.'

'A team in Naples.' The phrase had become familiar in his thinking. By the end of 1956, when he had been for twenty years in the American Methodist ministry, Casa Materna had passed through heavy storms. It had not only survived but was growing in influence. Though Papa was still in control, officially, much of the responsibility was being eased off his old shoulders by Teofilo, the doctor, and Fabio, the lawyer. Fabio had achieved a public eminence that had changed the whole status of Casa Materna in Portici and Naples. Teofilo was engaged in projects far outreaching the original scope of the orphanage. But while the external demands on Fabio and Teofilo were tremendous the needs of Casa Materna itself increased, too. 'A team in Naples' .... Emanuele could not rid his mind of the phrase. Against what might be no more than mere emotion he set the practical arguments of his bishop. 'You can do more good where you are!' It was odd how the long-past tension, the restrictions of Casa Materna in conflict with the freedom and self-expression represented by the United States, was becoming active once more. Now the maturity and discipline of these later years made the dilemma still more acute.

He waited, increasingly happy in the church at Castle Heights, and yet ill at ease, for anything that would resolve the conflict of loyalties. His sister Luisa, a great help in the American Casa Materna Society, was involved in her own family anxieties, for her husband Francesco was far from well.

Then, in October 1956, Emanuele received a letter from his brother Fabio in Naples. He held it in his hand for some minutes before he slit it open. His fingers trembled as he took it from the envelope. He found it almost impossible to see what was written and took off his thick glasses to wipe them. Every sentence stabbed him to the heart. The familiar beginning. '*Caro Emanuele* ... I shall very shortly be on my way to Rome ... we really do need you here in Portici ... what a team we could make together ... a doctor ... a lawyer who is also a politician ... a minister who is an educationalist.'

'A team in Portici.' The letter fluttered from his fingers as he began to sob. Emanuele knew now what he ought to do.

But he knew that it was already too late!

6

Fabio Outfaces Mussolini

THE political caution which kept Emanuele out of Italy was justified by events at Portici. Both on religious and political grounds Casa Materna became the target of Fascist attacks and it was due only to Fabio Santi's legal training and personal courage that its work was not brought to an end.

Benito Mussolini, in his early revolutionary days, once published a study of the fourteenth-century Bavarian religious leader, John Hus. After his rise to power copies of the book were destroyed, but sufficient remain to prove that at this period he was certainly not merely anti-evangelical but anti-religious. This, nevertheless, did not prevent his making a *volte face* at a decisive moment of his career and claiming the support of both King and Church.

The *Fasci*, black-shirted and arrogant, were extreme nationalists and began to spread their poisonous philosophy of violence even before the National Socialists came to power in Germany. While Adolf Schickelgruber, known to history as Hitler, was still scheming to use the German leaders for his own ends, Mussolini had already become *il Duce*, 'the Leader' of Italy. Both men were megalomaniacs, but while Hitler made conquests far beyond those of Mussolini's colonial empire it was *il Duce* who showed the way. From the suspect groups of *Fasci* he thrust himself quickly to the front of the Movement. Before the 1920s he was already a man to be reckoned with and he made it seem, to the poverty-stricken Italian people who had gained so little from the First World War, as well as to some of the leading industrialists, that the policies he advocated would bring prosperity and leadership to a nation left too long on the unprofitable verge of European political life.

In October 1922 he was appointed Prime Minister of Italy by King Victor Emmanuel III. A month later he assumed the powers of a dictator with the support (which could then scarcely be withheld) of the King himself and the qualified approval of the Roman Catholic Church, of which he now proclaimed himself a loyal member. In 1929 he ended the long breach which had existed between Church and State since the days of Garibaldi and Cavour by the signing of the Lateran Treaty. Pope Pius XI declared Mussolini 'persona grata' and, for his part, *il Duce* pledged his Fascist supporters to become the 'secular arm of the Papacy', vowing to destroy all opposition to it.

With the hindsight of our time it is easy to condemn the tolerance of the king and the compromise of the Papacy, but opposition to Mussolini by the king might have involved danger to the throne, and for the Papal Curia to try and exercise more than a moderating influence might have proved more disastrous for it than the *Risorgimento* in the last century. To the common people Mussolini promised great things and, in the physical and material realms, some of them were achieved, though only at the cost of a terrible evil which almost destroyed the whole nation. To the Church the dangers of the time seemed to be Liberalism, Communism and the Evangelicals. Mussolini was shrewd enough to gather the forces of the Church behind him in attacking all three, recognising more clearly than the Vatican that they were a far greater danger to Fascism than to the Church. Though it was not from any religious motive that he determined to exterminate all three groups his policy encouraged the latent hostility to the Evangelical Liberals.

In Naples an early example of this outcropping of buried enmity was the promulgation of a Pastoral Letter by the Cardinal of Naples against Casa Materna itself. Except for the current political climate it would have seemed a small target for such a notable authority to aim at. The Letter was known as *Timeo Danaos et dona ferentes*, a quotation from Virgil all the more apt since Virgil's tomb had for centuries been one of the 'sights' of Naples. 'I fear the Danai most of all when they bring gifts' was expounded to show that the apparently disinterested service of Casa Materna to poor and orphaned children was no more than a means of undermining the Catholic Church. A reply, drawn up by Riccardo Santi and Pastor Nitti, and published by the Evangelicals of Naples, may not have been of much effect as a counterblast but serves to draw attention to Riccardo's close association with Naples Protestantism and especially with the Nittis. This last fact was soon to be of significance. If Riccardo's position as the Principal of Casa Materna was a vulnerable one it was made all the more dangerous because of his association with the Nittis. Pastor Nitti was the father of a notorious 'rebel'.

Protestants, Liberals and Communists were persecuted and occasionally 'liquidated' by the Fascist State because their independence of thought was always a danger to an authoritarian regime, but also because of their foreign associations. Methodists, Baptists and Pentecostals all drew support from America, the traditional home of democracy. Liberals and Communists had lines of communication with Russia, America, Britain and other anti-Fascist countries. Casa Materna, in particular, was linked with the U.S.A.

Amongst those who belonged to the Evangelical-Liberal group in Naples were the Roselli brothers and Giuseppe Nitti. They were arrested, tried by a Fascist court, and imprisoned on Lipari, an island between Sicily and the toe of Italy reserved for political prisoners. 'Shot while escaping' from Lipari had a sinister meaning which was to become tragically familiar. Of most of those who 'escaped' nothing was ever heard again.

The news, splashed in the press, that Giuseppe Nitti and the Rosellis, 'notorious traitors to the Government', had escaped from Lipari brought more anxiety than hope to their friends. As soon as it was made public Riccardo Santi visited the Nittis, now in his old home, to commiserate with them. Ostensibly he went for another reason—to enquire after the health of Signora Nitti who was slowly dying from Parkinson's disease. There was no news of Giuseppe. He returned to Portici sad for this additional burden on an anxious family, though he would have been still more anxious had he realised that he had been followed from Naples back to Portici. From the moment of his visit to the Via Cimbri, Riccardo, like the Nittis, was under surveillance by the Fascist police.

A few weeks later there was a small parcel in the Casa Materna mail. It was obviously a book. The cover bore a French stamp and it had been posted in Paris. Riccardo ripped it open, curiously, and was even more surprised at its contents, a religious volume of no great interest. As the pages riffled through his fingers a piece of paper slipped out. The name of the sender, perhaps? A moment later he was running from the room, calling for his wife.

The letter was no more than the briefest of notes. *Let my Mother and Father know I am safe and well.* It was signed *Giuseppe Nitti*.

'But why send it to you?' demanded Mamma.

'Because if it had been sent to the Nittis the secret police would have opened it first!' Riccardo was already getting ready to go out. 'I must go and let them know.'

'Won't that be dangerous for you, too?'

Riccardo shrugged. 'They must be told.' With the folded note in his pocket he set off for Naples, trailed by a watcher on the tram and in the street. The Nittis were overjoyed.

'I shall die in peace,' murmured the signora. 'But what about you, Riccardo? They may have seen you come here. They watch everybody.'

'Don't worry about me. I'm of no consequence to the Fascisti,' replied Riccardo as he set off home to Portici.

Three weeks later Signora Nitti died, tranquil in the knowledge of her son's safety. But Riccardo had already been arrested. Almost as soon as he returned from Naples the Fascist police burst into the house. In the years that followed there were to be many more visits; seldom by the local *carbinieri*, almost always by the secret police.

The black-shirted captain glowered at Riccardo. His first question showed there would be no chance of prevarication.

'You had a parcel this morning?'

'Yes.'

'From Paris?'

'Yes.'

'What was in it?'

'A book.'

'What sort of book.'

'I will show you.' Riccardo picked it up and handed it across the desk.

The officer threw it down without interest. 'There was a letter in it.' It was a statement, not a question. 'Who was it from?'

'It was just a short note from the man who sent it to me.'

'Don't try any clever tricks with me, Santi.' Riccardo felt his hand tremble and moved it off the desk. 'Why did you go to Naples this morning? To the Nitti's house?'

'To enquire after Signora Nitti's health. She is dying of Parkinson's Disease.'

'Very friendly of you.' There was a sneer on the officer's face. He leaned over the desk and rapped on it with his revolver. 'The book contained a letter from Giuseppe Nitti. Where is it?'

Riccardo could only tell the truth. 'It is destroyed.'

'Very probably—and very unwise of you. What did it say, Santi? You'll find it easier to tell us now than after you've been interrogated in the cells.'

Riccardo blanched. 'It said he was safe and well. He asked me to tell his parents.'

The officer waited and his silence itself threatened more than words would have done. 'What else?' he demanded at last. 'Where is he? What was his address? Who was with him? What were his plans?' The questions rattled out, staccato and brittle. When Riccardo insisted that he knew no more the atmosphere grew more tense. For hour after hour the interrogation went on, hovering between violence and persuasion. At last the officer stopped the interminable questions and turned to his subordinates who had been lounging in the corner of the room. 'Take him away,' he snapped. 'If he won't answer here he'll answer at headquarters.'

Mamma watched in terror as her husband was dragged off to the waiting car and called the whole family to prayer as soon as it disappeared along the Corso Garibaldi.

The next morning Riccardo returned, shaken but unharmed and free. He had been interrogated throughout the night and threatened with imprisonment, but in the end the Fascist police had apparently accepted that his account of Giuseppe Nitti's note was true. But from that moment Riccardo Santi was marked out as an enemy. Spies were always in his congregation. More important, 'Casa Materna' became a file under Mussolini's own hand, to be opened when the moment for its destruction arrived.

* * * * *

With its political life dominated increasingly by the two dictators, and the democratic nations blindly or blithely unwilling to act realistically, Europe moved inevitably towards war. In 1933 Hitler was created Chancellor by Hindenburg. A year later he became Dictator of the Reich, consolidating his position by those acts of violence, distortion and mass-propaganda which Mussolini had used with such powerful effect in Italy. Soon Mussolini found himself playing jackal to Hitler's hyena tactics. Austria, to which Italy had laid claim for centuries, was occupied by Nazi troops. The Rome-Berlin Axis almost broke. The two dictators met in angry conference on the Brenner Pass, but it was Hitler who dictated terms. Until his terrible death Mussolini was to trail behind him, to lose the power of direct action, to drag his reluctant country late into war only to capitulate eighteen months before Hitler finally died in his bunker at Berlin. His own conquests of Abyssinia and Albania were trivial by comparison with Hitler's domination of Europe.

At home, however, *il Duce* tightened his grip on the Italian people. The Fascist police were feared throughout the country, and with reason. Those on their secret lists were always in danger, and the most trivial incident could bring them within sight of inprisonment or death.

Riccardo Santi was to become increasingly aware of this.

After the Nitti incident Fascist spies were seldom absent from the congregation, though they found little to report to their masters. For ten years, as Europe grew more troubled, regular visits were made by the police to Casa Materna. Much worse were the more irregular visits from the Fascist officers who questioned and interrogated until every small incident was made to seem like possible treason to the State. Probably it was Riccardo Santi's very ingenuousness which saved him more than any thing else. Letters were read, parcels opened, telegrams scanned, the telephone tapped.

It was a telegram which almost sent him to prison. On his birthday a friendly pastor sent him a telegram of greeting and, with customary piety, invoked a blessing on him by quoting a Biblical reference. Book, chapter, verses, no more.

Almost immediately the Fascist police arrived at Casa Materna.

'You are a spy,' they shouted.

Riccardo smiled gently. 'Nonsense. Who am I spying for?'

'You receive telegrams in code giving secret information.'

'That is absurd. This is a telegram of Christian greeting.'

'Then what is this? *Thess*? And these figures. *v*. And 23. They are a code by which you get messages from the enemies of the State.'

'Have you got a Bible?' asked Riccardo.

'What do we want with a Bible? We are not interested in Bibles, only in spies. You will be taken to Headquarters to explain.'

'But *Thess* means Thessalonians.'

'There is a figure in front of it. *I*. Explain that!'

'It means the First Epistle of Paul to the Thessalonians. The rest mean chapter 5 and verse 23.'

The secret police grinned in disbelief. 'You are a spy, Santi. You can try and explain these things away to the Major at Headquarters. He won't believe you, either. It would be better for you to tell the truth! And tell it quickly before you are hurt.'

Riccardo went confidently enough. But it cost him a night in the cells and long hours of interrogation before his explanation was accepted, grudgingly and with ill-temper that he had not been caught out at last.

* * * * *

By 1938 tension was almost reaching breaking-point. If Hitler's intention of annexing Czechoslovakia were opposed by the British and French Governments Mussolini and his Fascist leaders knew that war was inevitable. The pressures on groups or individuals with affiliations outside Italy became increasingly heavy.

At Casa Materna the schools had grown in size and influence. A couple of hundred children attended, both from the wealthier families of Portici, who readily paid for this privileged education, and from the poor, who could not get their children into the overcrowded state schools. In the orphanage there were about a hundred children, and the villa had been extended. Papa Santi was by this time an elderly man, sixty-six years of age, worn with long years of responsibility but far from worn out. His dark clothes hung loosely on his tiny frame and he moved less quickly than he used to. Yet, because there was no place on the budget for 'luxuries' he still cut the boys' hair and continued to act as their physician until after Teofilo had qualified as a doctor in 1933. His medical care was simple and specific.

FABIO OUTFACES MUSSOLINI

When Teofilo suggested new methods his reply was brisk. 'Castor oil has been good enough for the last thirty-seven years,' he asserted. 'It's the best thing in the world for cattle and children —and everybody knows it!'

By this time, however, Teofilo was an army doctor and Fabio, at twenty-seven, two years younger than Teofilo, a qualified and busy lawyer. Teofilo, despite his army duties at the Port, maintained a private practice at the villa, and both the brothers lived at home and shared Papa's administrative responsibilities. Now that Francesco Zaccaro was moving to the United States with the headquarters of his shipping company Luisa, too, was planning to return to Portici with her daughters.

It was at this point that the heavy hand of authority was thrust more violently into their family affairs.

One morning in 1938 a car skidded to a standstill outside the portico of the villa. The children stopped playing as four or five men leapt out and marched into the building. It was only a few minutes later when they saw their beloved Papa hustled out of the house and thrust into the car. A grim, black-shirted man stood with his hand on his revolver-holster until the doors of the car were shut, then jumped on to his motorcycle and roared away up the path between the trees after the car.

Papa's arrest found the whole family united at Portici and prepared to fight in his cause, although they had sufficient experience of the twisted processes of the law under Fascist pressure to know that intervention might be difficult and costly. The real trouble, as they saw the car drive away, was that they had no idea what charge might be preferred against him.

The most obvious one was of liaison with such democratic nations as America, Switzerland or Britain. Since considerable funds came from the U.S.A. this might not be difficult to prove to the satisfaction of a biased court. The Fascists, however, were shrewd enough not to alienate American sympathy unless it were eventually proved inevitable. An accusation of plotting against the State was more likely, or merely of espionage without specifying for what nation he was working. Either of these charges could keep him in gaol indefinitely, pending a full trial *in camera*, and during that time it might be possible to get rid of Casa Materna since Papa was nominally responsible for it.

The family's fears for Papa's safety were not groundless. Before he left the villa one of the Fascist police took Teofilo aside.

'You had better come, too, doctor. Your father will be taken to the police station and lodged in the cells in Portici. Bring some of his clothes with you.'

'Can I talk to him?'

The man shook his head. 'No. That won't be permitted. He will be tried tomorrow morning. You won't be able to go into the court but you can see and hear what is happening if the doors are open.'

Teofilo was glad Mamma was not within hearing. 'What *will* happen? What is the accusation?'

'I don't know. But it is likely he will be taken away. You may be able to see him then and give him such clothes as he needs.'

Next morning Riccardo Santi's name was called with about thirty others. It was the habit of the Fascist police to hide their victims amongst a normal group of criminals and to report to the Press that certain people had been gaoled. Under the general catalogue of 4 prostitutes, 3 thieves, 1 case of assault, 1 case of preaching strange doctrines, 3 cases of burglary, it was easy to dispose of potential enemies of the state without undue fuss or publicity.

Teofilo sat outside the door of the court as the first four cases were dealt with. The fifth was his father and Teofilo saw him face the two Fascist officers on the magisterial bench with complete calm. He was unshaven and his clothes crumpled.

'Riccardo Santi,' read the clerk of the court, 'you are accused of preaching strange doctrines.'

Teofilo heard the charge without relief. It was a familiar one. Some of the most notable Evangelicals, avowedly Liberal and anti-Fascist, had already been so accused and suffered imprisonment, disappearing completely from public life.

The officers leaned forward and the questions began.

'Who are you?'

'What is your occupation?'

'How long have you been in Portici?'

'How many children are there in your orphanage? In your schools?'

'What do you do in your orphanage?'

Every time Papa tried to answer a question at length he was silenced. Then came a question to which a longer reply could not be avoided.

'What do you preach?'

Papa put his hand in his pocket and pulled out his Bible. 'Listen.' His tone was that of a man who had been preaching for nearly half a century. 'I will tell you what I preach.' He opened the Bible and began to read. The Gospels . . . the Epistles . . . back to the Gospels. . . . As he read he broke off after each verse, sometimes after each phrase, to expound his Evangelical doctrine.

The presiding officer interrupted time after time. Papa made the same reply. 'No! You want to know what I preach and I must tell you. There is more than this!'

'Stop it at once!'

'There is more yet,' replied Papa, firmly, and went on before the general could swallow his anger and interrupt again.

What had begun as an inquisition had been turned into a preaching-service. Papa, thought Teofilo, is no longer in the dock; he is in the pulpit! Before all was ended it had turned, in the minds of many listeners, into comedy, too—the sort of comedy all Italians enjoy, in which the villain of the play is made ridiculous by the simple, honest man he has chosen as his victim.

The officer crashed his clenched fist on the desk before him. 'Stop! Stop this at once! Be silent!' The furious admonition was directed as much at the courtroom as at Papa Santi. It was seldom that the court, with its routine of pimps, prostitutes and common criminals, had the pleasure of seeing high authority outfaced so effectively. Then, as Papa put his Bible in his pocket, the presiding general made his last mistake. Up to this point it might have been possible to convict Papa of 'strange', or at any rate, anti-fascist doctrines from his exposition of the Scripture. His next demand lost the judge the day.

'What else do you do besides preach, Santi?'

Papa stared at him, as though astonished that he should be given yet another opportunity of declaring his faith. Then, quietly, in tones far gentler than his preaching voice, he replied, 'I pray.' He put his hands together. 'Like this!' He closed his eyes. 'Listen. I will show you how we pray at Casa Materna.' While the officers stared, for the moment uncertain what to do . . .

while Teofilo, outside the courtroom, felt himself transported to the intimacy of the Casa Materna family... as the police and the officials stood silent and immobilised... in the midst of criminals and women of no virtue, Papa Santi talked with God. He prayed at length and with deep earnestness. The children of Casa Materna, the poor people of Portici, those who were on trial that day, the rulers of the nation, the magistrates themselves, all these and many more had a place in his intercession... God's love for men and man's desperate need of God were laid open... the gentle daily mercies of God and His great deliverances were made subjects for thanksgiving. With a resounding 'Amen and Amen' he came, at last, to an end.

His eyes opened and he dropped his hands, turning from Heaven to the officers on the bench. 'That,' he said quietly, 'is how we pray in Casa Materna.' He had been praying for ten minutes.

Outside, Teofilo waited tensely for the verdict. It came with a roar from the presiding officer, as he half-rose to his feet, his swarthy face darker still with anger. All dignity had left him.

'Throw this man out!'

Back at Casa Materna Papa and Teofilo described what had happened. Teofilo's vivid account drew laughter and admiration for Papa's simple skill in discomfiting the court. But it was Papa who had the last word, as he had done in the courtroom. He was exultant, but not only because he had been acquitted.

'I have had an opportunity that comes to few of us,' he said. His face shone with gratitude. 'By allowing me to be arrested God has given me a chance of witnessing for Him to the Fascists. These irreligious men put themselves right in God's hands.' He gathered the children with his bright eyes and a gesture of his arm. 'Let us thank God, all of us, for this opportunity of speaking for Him.' Once more he closed his eyes and began to pray, commending to God the witness he had made in the Fascist court.

But, amongst the children, even the smallest was thanking God for something more personal, for the safe return of their beloved Papa to those who loved him.

Next day, when prayers would normally have been held in the schoolroom, Papa made an announcement. 'The Fascists wanted to know what we did; how we worshipped. They will certainly send their spies to see if what I said was right. It would be a pity

FABIO OUTFACES MUSSOLINI

if they had to creep round to try and listen at the windows.' The children laughed at the thought. 'From now onwards we will have our worship outside, on the verandah, where everyone can see and hear us without trouble.' He moved towards the door and the children followed him, gathering on the portico under the pillared roof. His voice raised, he began to read the Bible and then called them to prayer.

As he read he looked round the garden. Under the trees two men watched and listened. The spies were there.

* * * * *

In 1939, after a dozen years of hostility and interference, came the climax. A new charge was levelled at Papa.

'Riccardo Santi, pastor of the Methodist Church in Portici, is accused of putting a crucifix on the floor and teaching the children of Casa Materna to spit upon it.'

Mussolini himself at last opened the file labelled *Casa Materna*.

The accusation was wildly malicious, and made only as an excuse for the action which immediately followed. The Fascists were following their normal perverted course of acting on statements which no one was likely to believe but which, equally, no on would have the courage to contest.

In this case, however, they reckoned without the courage and tenacity of a twenty-seven year old lawyer, Fabio Santi.

As soon as the accusation was made a detachment of *carbinieri* from Portici marched through the gateway on the Corso Garibaldi. The officer laid a letter on the desk. 'Signore Santi,' he said formally, 'Casa Materna is closed. You are to get rid of the children at once.'

'Closed?' Papa stared at him. Now that the moment had come he could not believe he had heard rightly.

'Yes. Closed. All of it. The schools and the orphanage. It is to be disbanded at once. We shall take over the buildings.' The officer pointed to the paper. 'Read the letter. It is all there. Orphanage and schools. It's no use trying to argue. It is signed by *il Duce* himself!' There was no doubt about it. Mussolini had not left this to any deputies. 'We shall give you a day or so to get rid of the children, but no more.' The policeman turned on his heel and marched out.

When Fabio Santi returned from his office that day it was

evident that something was very wrong indeed. Papa's lined old face had lost some of its colour. He looked sick, and more than his age. Even Mamma made more noise than usual in the kitchen, surrounding herself with a surprising air of incoherence and purposelessness. There was little point to writing letters, checking stores, planning ahead through the week when the children would all be gone before it ended. The news was soon told and, for a rare moment, Fabio's natural ebullience left him.

Fabio was large in build, immensely so for an Italian from the south. Everything about him was big—his frame, his head, his voice and his laugh. Now, as he slumped on to a chair that looked too flimsy to support his weight, he seemed to grow smaller, looser, to have lost his customary optimism.

'Fabio will know what to do!' Papa's assertion, made so many times when things were difficult and reiterated today, seemed less true than usual.

'We can't do anything?' asked Papa.

'If it had been the local Fasicst headquarters it might have been possible. But we can't take the case higher than Mussolini himself.' Fabio reached over to the desk. 'Let me see that paper again.' He read it again, immobile, only his legal mind moving swiftly. Suddenly he leapt to his feet. 'It is *just* possible.' He crashed a huge hand onto Papa's desk. 'He can close the school; there's no doubt about that. But the orphanage... I think he's so eager that he's made a mistake. But whether the Courts will dare to say so is another matter.'

'What mistake can Mussolini make? He is a dictator. He can do anything!'

'You're wrong, Mamma.' Fabio's voice was excited. 'He prefers to maintain the forms of government. He won't alienate the people any further than he can help. Look!' He held out the closure order. 'He has signed this as Minister of Public Instruction.'

Mamma was still unimpressed by her son' legal attitudes. 'That means he is the final authority in education. He can close the school when he likes.'

'*Si, si!* Of course! He can close the *school* if he wishes. But not the Orphanage, *Mamma mia!* The Minister of Public Instruction has no authority over such things. It lies in the jurisdiction of the Minister of the Interior!'

Mamma was unconvinced. 'But is there anything we can really *do*?'

'Oh yes. I will lodge an appeal against the closure order on Casa Materna while I accept the closure of the school. I can say that I am preparing evidence concerning an error in the Order.'

'Will they take any notice of that?'

'Certainly. It will hold it up for a while, anyway. We can make arrangements for the children to be received elsewhere, perhaps, while we see what is going to happen. Not all Italy is Fascist. There are those in high places who still love freedom. The professors of the universities—they're not all Fascists. Nor are all the judges!' He put the paper in his pocket. 'May I take this? I shall lodge my appeal and go and see my Professor at the University tomorrow morning.'

Fabio's old Professor of Civil Law at Naples was a Jew, and as the young lawyer propounded his case he clasped his hands judicially. 'Yes,' he nodded, 'I believe you have a case, Fabio. Not a strong one. They may throw it out. But it *is* a case we can take to the courts. I will give you all the help I can in preparing it.' He stared hard at his young friend. 'But it could be dangerous —to you, personally. It means opposing *il Duce*, and that is something no man should do without forethought.'

'I'll risk that if it will save Casa Materna.'

During the rest of the year Fabio travelled between Naples and Rome two or three times a month, urging his right of appeal in the Roman courts. Leave to appeal was finally granted and the hard core of Fabio's case exposed. He immediately served a legal process on Benito Mussolini as Minister of Public Instruction for illegally issuing a decree for the closure of the orphanage.

To the onlooker what followed often seemed no more than a legal wrangle. To the High Court it was a matter of maintaining the integrity of the law against both official intolerance and private compassion. To Papa and Mamma Santi it was a matter of life and death for themselves and a hundred children.

'It will be a long case,' warned the High Court judges.

'The longer the better,' thought Fabio.

Every item of evidence was carefully sifted, from the finding of Angelo and Rosetta to the acquisition of the Villa Monaco and the present activities of Casa Materna. Riccardo's title to the villa and his standing as an Evangelical pastor were scrutinised. Month by month the case advanced.

From time to time the local *carbinieri* appeared, demanding that the orphanage be closed. On each visit they were politely informed that the court had not yet given its ruling. Then, on 10th June, 1940, the press and the radio carried news of far more public significance than the fate of a hundred children.

Italy had declared war.

In North Africa and on Italy's eastern front her soldiers and airmen went into action, and the departure of men on active service gave Fabio a new argument in the courts. 'These children's fathers need us to care for their children.'

'You must prove such a statement,' insisted the judges.

Fabio sent to every child's father who could be traced in the armed services. It took many weeks to assemble the replies, but when they were collected and taken to Rome their appeal was almost unanimous.

'Let my child stay.' 'You must continue to care for Pietro.' 'Casa Materna should not be closed.' 'If *Il Duce* will take my son into his own warm palace and keep him, clothe him and feed him while I fight his battles here on the Eastern front, he may go. Otherwise he is to stay with you.'

The letters were solemnly read aloud and noted.

The war came closer to Italy and Naples itself was bombed.

The following day the *carbinieri* at Portici themselves ordered the immediate closure of the orphanage. They were not prepared to be responsible for so many children gathered together in one place, and assured Papa that their order was concerned only with public safety and not at all with the case being heard in Rome. Fabio nodded in agreement, promising to come to the office the following morning to discuss the children's future. Papa looked astonished. His astonishment was small compared with that of the *tenente* of the *carbiniere* the next morning.

Along the Corso Garibaldi trooped a long procession of a hundred children led by Fabio Santi. He did not pause until he reached the police-station. There, he led the children into the outer office until it was completely full, and then flung open the door of the inner room where the lieutenant of police sat at his desk. He walked in, the rest of the children thrusting inside with him. The whole building seemed to be full of boys and girls.

The officer leapt up furiously. 'Get these children out of here at once,' he bawled.

Fabio spread his huge hands in a gesture of resignation. 'Impossible, *tenente*. Casa Materna is closing because of the war. They are not our children. You are closing the orphanage and they are all yours.' He made to leave the room, pushing his way through the wide-eyed boys and girls. '*Arrividerci, tenente!* Look after them carefully.'

The officer gulped and his sergeants managed not to laugh. 'Don't be ridiculous, Signor Santi! Where am *I* to put them?'

'That is *your* affair, not mine.' He was almost out of the door as he spoke.

'Come back, *signore*. How can I work with a hundred children round my feet? *Dio mio!* Take them back at once and don't bother me any more!'

The local skirmish was won. The battle in the High Court went on for months. In the end its conclusion brought victory to neither side, though the Santis were to continue to keep the ground they held. The compromise which emerged from the long and masterly judicial summing-up gave them as much as Fabio had ever dared to wish for and more than he had hoped. It gave the judgement to Mussolini while at the same time it immobilised the Fascists of Portici and Naples.

'In view of the situation caused by the war there is a great need of such places as Casa Materna where children and especially those who suffer through the war can be cared for. It must be closed when the war ends. Until that time it is to remain open, with Pastor Riccardo Santi in charge of it.'

The decision to close it when the war ended was carefully registered and not forgotten. But before the war was over Casa Materna and Italy itself were to experience new and acute hardships.

7

War Comes to Calabria

SOON after Mussolini's instruction to his Fascist police to close Casa Materna Poland was invaded by the Nazis. Two days later, 3rd September, 1939, Britain declared war on Hitler's Germany. At once there was uncertainty about Italy. British warships crowded the Gibraltar harbour and waited for orders in Malta and Cyprus, but Italy remained neutral. Not until France capitulated in June, 1940, did Mussolini seize the opportunity he had been waiting for. On 10th June, 1940, he declared war on Britain and an already defeated France.

To the Santis, facing scarcity and fighting a legal battle in Rome to keep Casa Materna open, the news was appalling. Teofilo was already serving in the Italian Army as a doctor. Fabio, despite a physical disability, might possibly be called up for active service. Papa was almost seventy and his wife about the same age. The High Court's decision to allow the orphanage to remain open seemed an answer to prayer but still left them with the acute problem of how the children were to be fed, clothed and maintained. Prices were soaring. Food was scarce. Supplies of every kind were scanty. Money was scarcer still, despite the help which for a while still continued to come from the United States. Then, on 7th December, 1940, the Japanese attacked the American navy at Pearl Harbour and America, too, was at war. But not only with Japan. She was at war with Japan's two partners in the Rome-Berlin-Tokyo Axis, Germany and Italy. To Papa and Mamma the new situation was almost unbearable. Emanuele, their eldest son, was an American citizen. Luisa's husband, Francesco Zaccaro, was in America, too. And the United States was now an enemy of their own land.

The first year's casual bombing was no more than a warning to the Italian people of worse things to come, though amongst the bombs were some which fell in the gardens of Casa Materna—British and American aerial torpedoes and incendiaries.

To the Italians the news from North Africa was disquieting. Their initial advances through the British positions were repulsed, and though the German troops under Rommel regained the lost territory and threatened completely to overrun the allied positions, the new successes did not bring release to the thousands of Italian soldiers who had been taken prisoner. By the end of 1941 Abyssinia and Eritrea were lost to Mussolini and by 1942 the British Eighth Army was advancing once more across North Africa. Within a year their colonies there were to be captured and used as bases for an assault on the mainland. The irony of the situation was tragic. The average Italian had no love for Mussolini or the Fascist State. His heart was not in the war and he longed for 'liberation'. But every British and American success brought more bombing, more deaths, longer lists of prisoners, a greater certainty that the towns and villages of the South would soon be ravaged and broken. In Naples the first sporadic attacks were superseded by pin-point bombing. In a city so large and overcrowded every raid brought destruction to the cluttered houses and tenements and death or homelessness to hundreds of families. Increasing contingents of German troops were concentrated in the area.

At Portici the children were terror-stricken. Some were on the edge of nervous breakdown and their thin bodies showed how sharp were their privations. How Papa and Mamma managed to get food was something like a miracle. Without Teofilo and Fabio to help they might never have survived at all. Indeed, more and more of the responsibility for Casa Materna was beginning to fall on Fabio's shoulders and it was fortunate that he was not called up for active service and still lived at home. Teofilo, too, who was still stationed at the Port military hospital and was medical officer to the British prisoner-of-war camp at Capua, normally lived at Portici.

It was because of Teofilo's presence that deliverance came for the children.

The one thing Papa wanted to do was to get away from Naples, to remove the children to some place safe from aerial attack and from the fighting that might well come to the city if the British and Americans invaded. By simple faith he had proved throughout his life that God, his Father, looked after those who trusted Him, but he had never regarded religion as an insurance against calamity or disaster. He knew that God was most likely to aid those who matched their faith with self-help. Now, however, he could do nothing to help himself. He had failed to find anywhere that he could take the children for safety. The whole of Southern Italy was threatened. There were Germans everywhere, who commandeered food and buildings. The hills were occupied by roving partisan and guerilla groups, many of them Communists, who would never tolerate the hampering presence of a hundred children.

One night in May, 1942, there was a knock on the door at Casa Materna. An Italian Army officer introduced himself as Captain Bideri and asked for Captain Teofilo Santi.

'The matter is urgent,' he said, as he was taken into the living-room. 'I want Captain Santi to do something for my sister. She's seriously ill.'

Teofilo, who maintained his private practice alongside his military service, saw nothing extraordinary in the request at first. 'Where is your sister?' he asked.

'At Praiano.'

'*Praiano!*' Teofilo made a gesture of despair as he lifted his broad hands, the firm fingers that might have belonged to a surgeon or a musician thrust outwards in rejection. 'If it had been Portici ... Naples ... yes, I could have come. But not Praiano. My dear Captain Bideri, it is impossible.'

'But why? I have a car. We could be there in an hour or so, as long as there are no bombs or roadblocks. You could be at the Port by morning. My sister is seriously ill—and there's no doctor in a village like Praiano. Why is it impossible?'

Teofilo explained. Often he *had* to be away on night duty, but when he was free he tried to be at home to allow his parents some sleep. When there were air-raids or 'alerts' the children had to be got to a place of shelter. He was not prepared to leave his father with the responsibility for the children throughout the night as well as during the daytime.

Captain Bideri was sympathetic. 'Children shouldn't have to endure these things. Why don't you take them to a place of safety?'

Teofilo laughed, without humour. 'Who would want all these children to add to their own problems?'

'How many are there?'

'A hundred!'

Bideri looked startled. 'It's a big family, yes. But it's not impossible, Captain Santi. Why don't you bring them to Praiano? Nothing ever happens there. There may not be much food, but we can still catch fish—and there aren't any bombs either.' Teofilo was staring at him incredulously. 'You could come and see my sister and I would enquire while you examine her. We have a big house of our own and there is another belonging to the family a hundred yards away.'

Fabio, who had listened without comment to the extraordinary conversation, was already on his feet. His great voice dominated the room. 'Let's go, Teofilo. At once!' If something were to be done, with Fabio it must always be done at once. 'Get your bag. I'll tell Papa where we're going and be with you in a minute.'

A few moments later, with Teofilo already in the car, Fabio heaved his heavy body in beside Bideri, talking as he came. It was typical of him that within ten minutes he was chatting to the captain as if he had known him for years. Before they reached the Amalfi road they were friends.

In daylight the drive from Portici to Praiano is lovely, and the long, narrow, twisting path above the sea, known as the 'Amalfi drive', incredibly beautiful. At night, under blackout conditions, it was extremely dangerous, and even with Bideri driving, who knew every gradient and bend on the road, it took them a long time to reach the little village. Praiano is a tiny hillside village clinging to the rocks on the southern side of the Sorrento peninsula. Sorrento itself is known to millions of visitors. Amalfi, Ravello, Positano and Praiano, the towns and villages of the southern side, remained before the war the possession of the people themselves and the treasured holiday-places of the adventurous or the rich. Few villages, even amongst the mountains, offered such freedom from the hazards of war or bombardment.

Before dawn, while Teofilo was caring for the sick woman, Bideri and Fabio had found two houses where the children might perhaps be accommodated if the villagers agreed. When Teofilo returned to Naples to report for duty at the Port, Fabio remained behind to negotiate arrangements in Praiano. If Teofilo had not been able to help Bideri's sister the opportunity might not have come; if anyone but Fabio, with his impressive presence, his geniality, confidence and natural friendliness had tried to win the Praiano people to accept a hundred orphans into their already straitened economy, the result might well have been failure. As it was, at the end of two days he returned to Portici to organise the removal of the whole orphanage across the Sorrento peninsula to safety.

A day or so later, with the help of Teofilo and Bideri, three army trucks arrived at Casa Materna. The children, as excited as their predecessors had been twenty years earlier when they moved from Via Cimbri to Portici, scuttled to and fro, chattering shrilly, heaving baggage, bedding, cooking pots and anything else they could take towards the trucks. Then, as darkness fell, with Mamma in charge of one truck, Papa and Teofilo 'commanding' the other two, the little procession moved off. That there should be an air-raid alert during the night was inevitable and they heard the crunch of the bombs not far away as they sheltered under the trucks, but none fell near them. By morning, they were unloading in their new home.

Praiano, a little way from its better-known neighbour Positano down by the edge of the blue water, clutches against the hillside high above the sea. Its houses, mostly white with an occasionally wash of pink or yellow, rise above the road that goes on its way over the peninsula to Sorrento. Far down below Praiano village is the cove, a jagged inlet amongst the precipitous cliffs with a triangular beach of shale and sand. Drawn up on the sand or riding at rope's end at the entrance to the cove lie the fishing-boats, red, blue and green. Above the cove, beyond the road, is a grey viaduct, below which a hill-stream bursts down through the brushwood. Not more than a mile away is the Grotto dello Smeraldo, whose hidden green waters beyond the mouth of the cave are a local and less crowded rival to the Blue Grotto of Capri. From the houses of Praiano to the beach or the grotto there is no other road than some three hundred steps.

Far across the bay, to the south-west, is the misty promontory of Cap Furore, an identifiable point in the stormy story of Virgil's *Aeneid*, while between the Sorrento promontory and the cape lie the town and far-stretching beaches of Salerno. Between Praiano and Salerno, so soon to play a bloody part in the war, were the villages of Minore and Majore, near neighbours of Praiano, and, nearer to Salerno, the lovely towns of Amalfi by the coast and peaceable, isolated Ravenna in the hills.

Amidst all this beauty the hundred children of Casa Materna were to spend the next two years; for Italy, the worst months of the war. In two houses, crowded together but free from fear, they lived under the supervision of Papa's own family. One house, a building with three arches across the verandah, its walls a deep siena, held Mamma, Luisa and the girls. The other, much bigger, jutting above the hairpin bend in the village, was needed for Papa and the boys. There were always more boys than girls in the orphanage, and there still are.

Each day began with prayers, held on the verandah of the girls' house, and there was school each morning under Luisa's supervision. In the afternoon there were rambles and scrambles round the hills, a long and cheerful race down the steps to the grotto or to the cove where the fishermen tended their nets before the night's fishing. On Sundays, Papa conducted an Evangelical service on the verandah and, a few at a time, the villagers came to listen.

It was not all, however, as idyllic as the description suggests. In the beginning the villagers, despite their concern for the children, were hostile and afraid, certain that the advent of so many Protestants into a Catholic village would bring them ill-luck. But, as the months of war came and went and Praiano remained almost the only place on the peninsula not to be bombed or attacked in any way, they began to ascribe their safety both to the special care which God accorded to these children and to their own piety in sheltering them.

But other difficulties were not so simply solved. In particular, food was always a problem. It was here that Fabio, who spent as much time as he could in Praiano, was so greatly useful. He saw to a fair division between villagers and children, made sure that fish was available—at any rate once a week—and comforted the children when there was nothing else but beans, which normally would be fed only to horses, with a few chestnuts to give them savour. Fabio's visit became as welcome to the village as to Casa

Materna. Because he was a lawyer endless disputes and problems were brought to him to solve: because he was the humane person he was, more intimate concerns were shared with him. Before their stay was ended he had become accepted as 'the little mayor of Praiano', a slightly comic title for so big a man.

When he was not at Praiano Fabio continued to live at Portici and work in Naples. It needed more than legal skill, however, to preserve the Casa Materna property from those who had their eyes on it. True, the heavy gates were closed firmly against intruders, but they could not be barred against the Germans. Once inside they took what they needed. It had been impossible to remove all the domestic goods to Praiano and by the time the 'family' moved back there was little left for them to use. Mattresses, kitchen utensils, crockery were filched by German soldiers and what they did not want was mostly pilfered by the poor people of Portici, to whom Fabio grudged it rather less than he did to the Germans. As Italian reverses continued in North Africa and the military threat to the continent of Europe increased, more and more Germans were concentrated round Naples. Their need for accommodation increased, and the villa at Portici, standing empty apart from the presence of Fabio and the occasional residences of Teofilo, could not escape their attention. Large unbombed premises in Naples were becoming scarcer as the bombers devastated it week by week.

This time it was Teofilo, not Fabio, who was to save Casa Materna.

It was in the summer of 1943 that a reconnaisance-party of German officers drove their car into the compound in their search for a new military headquarters. Teofilo was at home and walked to meet them in his trim medical uniform. With Teutonic brusqueness they introduced themselves and their business. Protests were useless and dissuasion seemed impossible. Teofilo explained that it was an orphanage but he could not pretend that it was being used by the children.

'It appears to be exactly what we are looking for,' said the major in charge of the party. 'The keys, please. We will find our own way!'

After examining the building by the main road they walked through the grounds to inspect the villa itself. Tramping into the house they left a young lieutenant in the hall with Teofilo. The two young men eyed each other warily. The lieutenant wandered round and stopped in front of a plaque on the wall of the entrance hall. His English was not good but he suddenly pointed to one word.

'*Methodist*. Why is that word there?' he asked.

Teofilo answered in German. 'Because the building for the orphanage was given by the Methodist Church in the United States.'

The soldier looked with new interest at Teofilo. 'You are a Methodist, Captain Santi?'

'Yes.'

The lieutenant clasped his hand with fervour. '*Ich bin auch Methodist!*'

'If you, too, are a Methodist,' answered Teofilo, 'try and save the property for me. If it becomes a German military site it will be bombed.'

The German clicked his heels and saluted. 'I will do what I can, Captain,' he promised and climbed up to the roof to join his senior officers.

A few minutes later the whole party came down the stairs. The major in command of it shook his head as he approached Teofilo. 'It is not as good as it seems. This young man has pointed out that the roadway between the two buildings is very obvious from the air. Camouflage would be difficult, too. It will be no use. A pity! It seemed just right.' He climbed into the car. '*Auf wiedersehn*, Kaptan Doktor!'

The car moved down the drive and Teofilo went back into the entrance hall to look once again at the plaque that recorded the American Methodists' generosity and to thank God for His intervention.

German artillery, anti-aircraft guns and troops poured through the city. Then, on 10th July, 1943, the British and American forces invaded Sicily. Italians were divided between fear for their own fate, hatred of the Germans, and a hope that if the British and Americans forced their way through Sicily they might soon free their country from the detested Fascists who had plunged them into war. Two months later Sicily was overrun, its towns smashed and its German and Italian forces dead, in retreat or taken prisoner. On 3rd September the invading forces crossed to the mainland.

War was coming very near to the frightened children in Praiano, and five days later it approached nearer still. Past Cap Furore steamed the invading fleet and British and Americans landed on the Salerno beaches and, nearer at hand, on the little beaches of Majore and Minore. The children were terrified. The bay, full of shipping; the reverberation of gunfire and explosions; the rattle of rifles and machine-guns amongst the nearby hills; the sky reddened at night by flashes, flares and fire; all these made it seem that their own destruction was only a few hours or days away. Their beloved Papa and Mamma would be killed. Where Uncle Fabio and Uncle Teofilo might be, as the fighting raged and the aircraft roared through the day and night to drop their bombs on Naples, they had no idea. From the hilltops they could see the dark mass of men fighting on the Salerno beachhead.

Then, slowly, quietness came to Salerno as the Germans retreated to occupy the bare hills between the coast and Naples itself. There, for a month, they harrassed and blitzed the army which slowly fought its way up the open valleys, driving out the Germans from each individual hill-top day by day.

But, for the British and Americans, the Germans alone were now the enemy.

Italy had capitulated on 8th September, 1943.

A month later, on 1st October, Naples fell. The partisans and guerillas in the hills became the allies of the invading forces. For the children, though not for Italy, the war was over.

'Can we go home now, Papa?' Scores of thin, ill-clothed boys and girls asked the same question when the news of the Italian armistice was broadcast. It took a long time for Papa to explain that Naples was no fit place for children and that it might be a long time before they would be able to settle down once more at the villa in Portici. Already Fabio had brought news of what was happening.

The Germans, determined to hinder the allied advance, had planned to mine the Casa Materna buildings and only the swift advance of their enemies had prevented them doing so. Now, with British and Americans pouring into Naples, every possible building in the devastated city was being taken over to serve as

WAR COMES TO CALABRIA

billets and offices. Casa Materna was occupied by British soldiers, for that sector of the city was under British control. The Americans were occupying other parts of the city in a joint Allied administration.

But, if Fabio brought bad news about the possibility of return, he brought good news, too. Soon after the allies entered Naples he brought friends as well.

One of his first acts was to go to the Allied Headquarters on behalf of the children at Praiano. Wisely, he did not waste the time of highly-placed officers who would have had little concern with a hundred children when the whole population was in despair. Instead, he sought out the Protestant chaplains, told them the wonderful story of Casa Materna and its deliverance and asked their help for the children and the villagers who had sheltered them. Their first reaction was sympathy, their next more cautious move to go and see for themselves what was happening. The loveliness of the Sorrento peninsula and the exquisite beauty of the villages on its southern side was refreshment indeed after the horrors of the last months of war and destruction. Surrounded by children who were intrigued to see for the first time what Americans in uniform looked like, battered by shrill questions in a language they could not understand, they had no more doubts. Here were children who needed help. They had no hesitation in promising to do what they could for them and their kindly hosts. Food from Allied canteens and kitchens was brought over the hills and the villagers of Praiano were amongst the first to receive help.

It was over a year later when the children were able to move back to Portici, in October 1944. The buildings, occupied by British soldiers, were in a terrible state of dilapidation and the gardens, once so lovely, were a jungle of weeds and rank grass. Room was made in the building near the road for the girls to sleep, but the boys had to find space in the barn by the old red farmhouse, in the garage or in tents which the soldiers erected in the grounds. Nothing was the same as it had been and outside, in Portici and Naples, destruction was appalling. Papa and Mamma wept at all they saw. To the children, with their clear eye for essentials, none of these things really mattered. Casa Materna was home again.

8

'The Protestant Doctor': Teofilo

A PROFESSIONAL guide (and they are very good) taking a party round Pompeii needs two hours to do so. Teofilo Santi, if he had the time, would fill every minute of a whole day and still not leave his companions bored. To see him taking a group of Casa Materna children round these ruined streets and villas, shops, arenas and temples is to see something very different from a master instructing his class or a guide picking out the high points of interest. Roman electioneering slogans painted nineteen hundred years ago on the walls . . . pedestrian crossings at the road-junctions . . . the marks of chariot wheels on the hard stone . . . empty water-pots at a wayside tavern . . . all these things and many more he uses to bring people to life again. Roads and villas become peopled with Romans at work, at play and in love. 'People' is a key-word in understanding Teofilo.

To walk round one of the great Naples museums with him, as I did through San Martino one morning, is to have the same experience. Historical paintings, military uniforms, playbills, the incredible crib with its own crowded landscape, he makes fascinating because of their personal associations. History, too, speaks to him of 'people'. In the same way, Latin and Greek are not dead languages but links with those who spoke them, while modern languages were never a school discipline but a means of communicating with people across frontiers. For Teofilo Santi 'people' are 'life'.

Dark, stocky, bright-eyed, from the beginning he was a contrast to his two brothers, themselves so different from each other. Emanuele, politically-conscious and music-loving, would readily desert his academic work for his violin. Fabio, always brilliant, seemed to reach the top of the class without working. Teofilo was both student and scholar, loving knowledge partly for its own sake but learning early to translate it into human terms. Religion, was, for him, a matter of personal relationships and he found it easy to accept a belief in God as a loving Father who must in many ways be very much like their own beloved Papa.

When Teofilo was sixteen and Fabio fourteen the links that tied the three brothers so closely together were broken. Emanuele left Italy for America. The consolation he offered his disappointed father was sincere, however, not a pious piece of self-deception.

'Teofilo will perhaps make up for it,' he had said, and Papa had smiled gently. It might well be, but Emanuele was his eldest son, the boy he had given in his mind and his prayers to the ministry.

For Emanuele there had always been only one vocation. Teofilo was trying to balance three different ones against each other. He had inherited his mother's musical ability, like Emanuele, and was an outstanding pianist. The Naples Conservatorio of Music was a real possibility. The thought of healing had always attracted him, though a medical career would seem to be out of reach of the poor boys of Portici. But, within a year of his older brother's departure, his mind was made up.

'I believe God wants me to be a minister,' he confided to his delighted parents.

'You will go to Rome,' said Papa. 'It is still our only Theological College.' He thought back thirty years through the past. 'You might even have the very room that I had.'

'If it's still there.' Mamma's sharp voice was practical, not dreamy. 'They say there's very little money these days for training ministers.'

'They couldn't close the College,' protested Papa. 'It *has* to be kept open!'

But, as was not infrequently the case, Mamma's realism was more accurate than Papa's dreamy optimism. America, caught like the rest of the world in the 'slump' of the mid-1920s, found less money available for its church budgets and especially its missionary commitments. To Teofilo and a few others who were hoping to train there the College in Rome sent the disappointing news that the Methodist Board of Missions in the United States had decided to close it down owing to lack of funds. Once more

Papa's high hopes were thwarted. More important, Teofilo, ready to leave school in 1926, had to rethink his future. He did it prayerfully, believing that if God had permitted one door to close He would lead him through the one he was meant to enter. Music? No. That was still to be no more than an occasional pleasure. Medicine? He went on praying, and his choice was made.

'If I can't be a minister, I'm sure God wants me to be a doctor,' he announced.

Papa looked uneasy. 'If you were a pastor there would be a church for you, somewhere. If you became a teacher you could find work in a state school. But a doctor—that's very different!'

'Why?'

'Where would you practise? Here in Portici? Naples?'

'Possibly.'

'No one would come to you. You're a Protestant, Teofilo, and there isn't a single Protestant doctor in the whole of Naples. You'd never be able to make a living. Doctors and priests work hand in hand.' It was a statement of fact, not a complaint.

The dilemma left him perplexed and frustrated. Clearly Papa was right. Yet the more he prayed about it the more certain he was that he was meant to be a doctor. In the end, he applied for admission to the Medical Faculty of the University of Naples, was accepted, and qualified there. For a while, after his graduation, he studied in Berlin and, because Italy had colonies in North and East Africa, specialised for a time in tropical medicine. In Lausanne, where he also spent some time, he enlarged his experience and interests, and made valuable contacts with Swiss Protestantism. Albert Schweitzer, with his idealism, his music and his hospital at Lambarene, so caught his imagination that for a while he considered becoming a medical missionary in the tropics. But, like Emanuele, he could not get children out of his mind. It was not really surprising. In Naples and Portici he had lived as one of an ever-expanding family and, apart from the brief periods he spent outside Italy, he was never out of reach of their voices. He prepared to specialise in paediatrics so that he might care for them more knowledgeably and effectively.

Once more the pattern of his life twisted. In 1933 he was called up to do his four years military service. As a private in the Army Medical Service he had to accept the dirty and undignified chores he had seen relegated to hospital orderlies for the past six years, but fortunately he was quickly commissioned as *lieutenente* and before the end of his national service promoted *tenente*. At the end of his conscripted service, in 1937, he decided to take a medical commission in the regular Italian Army. He remained in it until he was discharged after the war, at the time of the Italian armistice in 1943.

To those accustomed to the British or American military machine, however, Teofilo's Army service was unusual if not incredible. Instead of being posted from one hospital to another he remained throughout his whole service attached to the Military Hospital at the Port of Naples. Instead of having to live in a medical mess, he lived for almost the whole time at home in the villa at Casa Materna. More astonishingly, he was permitted to build up and maintain a private practice throughout his military career. Though he worked at the Military Hospital each morning and took his normal turns of duty, at other times he practised in his own surgery and went on his rounds during the afternoons and evenings. What it meant to Papa and Mamma during the war to have him at Casa Materna has already been seen in the previous chapter.

This telescoped summary of his career, however, has totally disregarded the hazards and heartaches which characterised the earlier part of it. Papa's contrary words proved only too accurate.

Nowhere is it easy for a young man to break into territory where other doctors are already at work. The only people likely to come to him at first are those who are disgruntled with the service or manners of their own doctors—and they are as likely to fall out with the new one as with the old. A newcomer's only hope, as a rule, is to become the junior partner in an established practice. To Teofilo the latter course was completely closed. No Catholic doctor wanted a young Protestant for a colleague and for months it seemed that no one was willing to risk having a Protestant as a medical adviser. By the time he qualified Casa Materna had been established at Portici for twelve years, but the old suspicion had not entirely died away. A new church had been built opposite orphanages and schools had been opened in connection with its work. Pious fears of its evangelical teaching were widespread though less outspoken.

There *were* patients, nevertheless, after a while, though they were not the sort a doctor looks forward to receiving, especially a young man in his middle twenties beginning his life's work. Some came because their own doctors could do no more to help. Others came because they had no money. All were incurable. After six years of hospital training it took very little time to diagnose pneumonia, cancer, acute bronchitis and tuberculosis. These, and only these, were the sad people who turned hesitantly into the patio at Casa Materna or summoned the young doctor to their squalid rooms. He eased suffering where he could but there were no spectacular successes to make his name ring round the alleys and courts of Portici. He did not expect to cure where men of longer experience had given up hope.

All the same, there *were* gains. Though he could not give healing he did give courage. Though a Protestant's prayers would have almost literally scared them to death, he spoke quiet words of faith. If no tales of miraculous healing spread through Portici, at least men and women began to talk of the new doctor's kindness, gentleness and compassion.

'He deals with patients like the pastor Santi himself deals with children—as if he loves them.'

That was, in some ways, a firmer beginning than some flash-in-the-pan wonder of recovery from seeming certain death. Yet it brought little comfort to Doctor Teofilo. Indeed there were days when he almost wept over his choice of a profession and nights when he prayed, nearly in despair, for a case that was curable. Then, in time, as a natural response to his reputation for compassion, they came. His gains were not spectacular. It was merely that a less desperate man or woman summoned him or brought a sick child who was not so completely beyond hope as those who had first sought him out. And, unknown to him, he was gaining a strange new reputation all his own.

A man knocked at the door at Casa Materna and stood, shifty-eyed and shuffling, on the threshold. 'You are the new doctor? I have a sick boy but nothing helps him. Neither the doctor nor my woman's prayers to Sant' Ciro.' He looked away, down the avenue to the sea, unwilling to meet the young man's eye. 'We've done everything and my woman is nearly mad with anxiety. "If God's own doctors can do nothing for the boy", she said, "why don't you go to the new one, the one that's in the pay of the devil?" So that's why I've come, *signore*. It doesn't matter to us if you *do* work for the devil if you can help my child!'

He was the first of many such strange visitors. Teofilo was resiliant enough to laugh at his reputation and young enough to be in touch with new medical knowledge. A report of his diabolic powers was likely to spread even faster than the rumour of his kindness, and he could rely on experience and time to counter such superstition, provided cases came his way and he was able to help. Now not all who came were beyond hope. New drugs and new techniques brought recovery where older men failed because they relied only on time-worn remedies and nostrums. Teofilo's reputation grew and his list of patients lengthened. It became more and more common for him to be called out at night or to find a group of black-clothed women, old and young, waiting for him when he returned from his duties at the Military Hospital. Instead of being known as the devil's servant he gained a new—though to some an equally sinister—title. He was 'the Protestant doctor'.

Outside Calabria and the South it might seem a strange definition, but in Naples in the 1930s it was entirely accurate. He *was* the Protestant doctor, the only one in the whole of Naples, and that alone was sufficient to make him famous—or notorious! One of those to whom he was indeed notorious was the priest of San Giovanni.

San Giovanni was a crowded, poverty-stricken parish lying between Portici and the Naples docks and the thought of a Protestant entering his people's homes so shocked the parish priest that he denounced Teofilo from the pulpit. It was an action by this time so rare that it quickly reached Casa Materna.

'The priest says you won't tell people they are dying so that they will die without the last rites of the Church.'

'The priest is an ignorant man,' asserted Teofilo to the little gossiping group in his surgery.

'But he says that you do this so that we Catholics will go to hell!'

'Then he is not only ignorant but wicked. I try to save lives, not to send innocent men to hell.' For once Teofilo was really angry at the malicious attack. 'Have you ever heard any other priest say this of me?'

The men and women shook their heads. 'They used to be against you in Portici, certainly. But not like that. And not now.'

Teofilo smiled, his eyes suddenly twinkling. 'No. We know each other better in Portici now. But, as for the priest of San Giovanni, I will see that he has no excuse for saying what he does.'

The opportunity for 'placating' his critic came sooner than he expected. Within a few days he was called out in the small hours to see a woman in San Giovanni. Threading his way through the narrow streets he came to a house with crumbling walls and overcrowded rooms. The relatives, all talking at once, expounded the story, the symptoms, their hesitation in calling him after what their priest had said. But not all doctors were willing to come to San Giovanni in the middle of the night, one man pointed out, brushing away the parish's reputation with a shrug and a sweep of his hands.

'And you needn't have pulled *me* out of bed at two o'clock in the morning, either,' thought Teofilo as he looked at the patient; 'there's not much wrong here!' But he did not say the words aloud. Instead, his face became solemn as he straightened up from the bed.

'Is it serious?'

Teofilo nodded portentously. 'It *might* be serious. You had better call the priest of San Giovanni.'

The relatives exchanged uneasy glances. 'But the priest said we were not to send for the Protestant doctor!'

'That's your affair, not mine. Why didn't you call someone else?' When there was no answer he went on. 'We must pray to God for help.'

The chattering stopped. The woman's eyes widened with horror. The more ignorant Neapolitan peasants in their sicknesses and difficulties speak naturally of 'praying to the saints'; 'to Mary the Mother of God'; even 'to Christ Jesus' in greater moments of stress. But God is far away beyond these intermediaries. Only in extremity does a Neapolitan say: 'we must pray to God!' That the doctor should urge this filled them with terror.

'We will go for the priest!' Two men were going out of the room as they spoke.

Teofilo had left for home before the priest came and did not hear the violent denunciations of the 'Protestant doctor' and those who had called him. But next morning when he called on the way to the Port Hospital the woman was already beginning to recover. When the priest called later in the day to see if she were dead she smiled at him gaily.

'He's a very good doctor,' she informed him. 'He brought me back from death!'

It was a few weeks later when Teofilo was summoned from bed to go again to San Giovanni. He shivered as he pulled his overcoat round him against the night wind. It would be unfortunate for the priest if he also had to come out on such a depressing night, he thought, chuckling to himself. This time it was a child he was asked to attend and, though for the child's sake he did not pull quite such a solemn face as previously, he still insisted that the priest be summoned. Grumbling about the weather—and Teofilo sympathised with him, for it was worse than ever—the priest hurried through the streets. As he bustled into the room, his thin fanatical face turned angrily for only a moment towards the doctor, the rain dripped from his cloak to the stone floor. By next morning the child was getting better.

On the third occasion a storm beat up across the Bay of Naples and filled the uneven, cobbled streets of San Giovanni with treacherous pools of water and filth. The small reflections of the street lights did little to brighten the night. Teofilo shivered as the husband of the sick woman on the bed opened the door to go and fetch the priest.

At the presbytery he told his story. His wife was sick . . . very sick . . . she might die before the morning.

'Who is your doctor?'

The man hesitated. 'I couldn't get one to come . . . I had to go to Portici . . . Dr Santi came at once . . . I know what you said, but. . . .' He got no further, for the door was already closing in his face.

'The Protestant doctor? Go home, man, go home! Why fetch me in the middle of a night like this?'

'But my wife?'

'I will come and see her in the morning. If you have the Protestant doctor the woman will live!'

Teofilo's ruse had not taken long to work. The priest's words were as good as a recommendation and they spread through his parish, and indeed through Naples, with the speed of an epidemic. There was no more preaching against him in the pulpit of San Giovanni.

Little by little, though seldom by such devious means, the opposition broke down. Teofilo's thick-set form became a familiar sight in the lanes and courts of Portici and the parishes that stretched into Naples. He had no need to look for patients; they sought him out and kept him busy till late at night. He is one of the few doctors—perhaps the only one—who has never put up a name-plate at the entrance to his home. Casa Materna and Teofilo Santi were equally well and widely known.

'Sant' Ciro has returned to Portici!'

The Santis had come a long way from the days when the people implored their patron saint, the good doctor of mediaeval days, to drive the heretics away. Now 'the Protestant doctor' seemed almost to be the reincarnation of their beloved parish saint. In Teofilo they found the compassion, the care, occasionally the almost miraculous skill which tradition ascribed to Sant' Ciro himself. Not only was Teofilo the doctor of the poor, however, and especially of the children; his name became more widely known. He was consulted by professors, called in to assist in hospital operations, sought out by patients from far outside Naples.

But Teofilo remains a member of the Casa Materna family, a Santi whose very name proclaims him an Evangelical, a man known to be a leader in Protestant circles throughout Italy. Unable to enter the Methodist ministry, he remained a devoted Methodist and became a lay preacher of that Church, exercising a preaching ministry in Portici, Naples and towns and villages of Southern Italy. He has been for many years a member of the Standing Committee of the Italian Methodist Church, and President of its Committee on Social Service. In 1961 he led a 'caravan' of Italian Methodists on a pilgrimage to England, touring the historic religious sites of the country.

The only one of the three Santi brothers to marry, his wife strengthened the family's Evangelical links, for Livia, whom he married in 1951—on the 50th wedding anniversary of his parents—was the daughter of an Italian Baptist pastor who had been a missionary in Tunis. He first visited her as a patient and, not surprisingly, was attracted by her grace and charm. A schoolteacher by profession, Livia Santi is devoted to the children of Casa Materna and works as hard for their welfare as does her husband. Indeed, because of his many other more recent commitments, much of the responsibility for Orphanage and Schools rests on her slim shoulders.

Probably the most important feature of 'the Protestant doctor's' work, in the long run, is that it has done so much to bridge the gap between religious communities in Portici. Inevitably Teofilo's patients include far more Catholics than Protestants, and this is taken for granted. They include local parish priests and he is official medical adviser to two convents. He plays a leading part in medical affairs in the city and works alongside other doctors, without any religious barriers, in schemes in which they are mutually interested. For five years he was a member of the Portici Municipality, where he had a special concern for the provision of the first town hospital, a scheme which his brother Fabio initiated. Not only was he a member of the Municipal Council but for two years he was also Deputy Mayor.

This situation, so different from the 1930s when he was attempting to establish himself in an alien and suspicious township, so incredible in the days when the Prince of Monaco sold his villa to the Evangelicals and then tried to buy it back again, so astonishing to Papa Santi who remembered the past all too vividly and found it difficult to come to terms with the present, owes much to the Christian love of good Pope John XXIII, in whose honour Dr Teofilo Santi delivered the Municipality's memorial oration. But, before the wind of change which has blown from the Vatican was so much as a zephyr reaching the outside world, the climate was changing in Portici. To this new local spirit of tolerance and understanding Teofilo the doctor and Fabio the lawyer probably contributed more than anyone else.

In this chapter our attention has been focussed on Teofilo as the doctor who lived at Casa Materna and had his surgery just inside its main gate. Nothing has been said of his experiences during the war or the work he did in the camps. His astonishing ventures in the 'caves', his pioneering settlement in the *barracche*, where it seems to the world at large that Dom Mario Borelli has been alone at work amongst the *scugnizzi*, and his last great ecumenical scheme in the Communist enclave of Ponticelli, must form the final chapters of this book. It would be proper to notice at this point, however, an honour bestowed on him by his own Church.

Methodism in Italy is but one small part of the wider Evangelical community, but it is now stronger than it has ever been, integrated and united. Work was begun at the time of Garibaldi's revolution, when religious liberty was guaranteed, by both the British Methodist Missionary Society and the American Methodist Board of Missions. Because Naples was under the supervision of the Americans Casa Materna received financial help from the United States from its early days. In 1946, however, the Americans withdrew from their work in Italy, and by agreement with Britain, all Italian Methodism came under the oversight of the British Methodist Missionary Society. A British minister, appointed to the English-speaking Methodist church at Port St Angelo near the Vatican in Rome, acted as a 'liaison officer' between Britain and Italy. Then, in 1963, Italian Methodism became an independent Church. Its leader, the President of the Italian Methodist Conference, is a minister, appointed annually. The Vice-President is a layman. In 1964, in the second year of its independent existence, Dr Teofilo Santi was appointed Vice-President, an office which involved him in wide touring and preaching activities throughout Italy and in representing the Italian Church at the Methodist Conference in England. Like the ministerial President, the Vice-President must deliver an address at the beginning of the Conference.

Teofilo Santi mentioned theological issues and the growing fellowship of all the Churches but it was natural that his main concern was with the social witness of the Church and with the contemporary debate on the place of the Christian layman in society. Those who heard did so with more than admiration or interest. His words stirred the Church because nowhere amongst the Evangelical Churches of Italy is there a layman with a more sensitive social conscience, who has involved himself with more selfless devotion in the needy world about him or shown more patently the compassion of the Christ he serves than Teofilo Santi, 'the Protestant doctor'.

9

The Lawyer: Fabio

IN the early days after the Santis moved from Naples to Portici comparatively few Casa Materna children went to high school. Teofilo and Fabio were amongst them, though there was no money for fees and they had to win scholarships to get there. In the evenings the high school children did their homework at the large table in Papa's own apartments. There was no chattering and no cheating; Mamma saw to that. A few wrote quickly, depending on the subject; more chewed ruminatively on their pencils, but one boy always finished first.

'Have you done it properly, Fabio?'

There was no real need for Mamma to ask the question. The others plodded, sought for inspiration, began again. Fabio seemed never to forget anything, leapt straight to the heart of a question, used words as if he were their master. The other three Santi children were far above average—there were few Italian families where doctorates were gained so freely—but Fabio was brilliant. He seemed to reach the top without trying and was born for success.

Nor was he good only at academics. Music he loved, like the rest of the family, but though he was Emanuele's pupil he never mastered either piano or violin. This, as Emanuele would explain swiftly, was the fault of Fabio's slightly twisted finger, not of his tutor. His compelling interest, however, was sport. Throughout his life, the children apart, he was seldom happier than when he was playing or watching football or athletics. On the football field his immense size made him a formidable opponent. Yet, strangely enough, he mixed more easily with older people than with those of his own age, following their discussions knowledgeably and making his own contribution without brashness. There was a maturity about him in his early teens that in some strange way contrasted with his youthful vigour and enthusiasm in his later years.

It was in his second year at high school that his whole career seemed to fall to pieces. It occurred because of his own stubborn regard for truth.

All Italian schools follow the same course and, for each subject, use the same text-book which is approved by the Ministry of Education. In the second year the history course included the Reformation. Since the teacher of religious history was a priest it would have been perfectly in order for Fabio to remain outside the classroom. Instead, he elected to stay in. The teacher gave dates, places, events, and the boys made notes in their books. Then he put the book down and began to speak of Luther. From the German reformer he moved on to Calvin, who made Geneva the headquarters of his reforming movement. His presentation of their characters was dubious and his anecdotes about them scurrilous. The class giggled and shuffled, turning to look at Fabio Santi, the one Protestant in the room. Casa Materna had been established for only a year or two in Portici and the teacher enthusiastically seized the opportunity of discrediting the heretics and their reforming founders.

Fabio sat upright, his big cheerful face grown grim and angry. He said nothing.

The following day the teacher began where he left off. Then, suddenly Fabio rose to his feet. '*Signore!*'

'Well, Santi?' The teacher was very smooth, apparently surprised at the interruption.

'Will you please keep to the book, sir!'

'What do you mean, you insolent boy?'

'It does not say those things that you are saying in the textbook. Your duty as a teacher is to teach what it says in the textbook, not to pass your own opinions.'

The teacher looked at him but instead of the fury the class expected he had only a sardonic smile. 'So you're a rebel, Santi? You're going to teach teachers how to teach? I doubt if we have room for rebels in this school, especially when so many other boys wish to come to it.' Fabio's face paled. 'Leave the room. I will speak to the headmaster about you.'

Before the morning session was over Fabio was sent home, to try to explain what had happened. Papa was inclined at first to rejoice that his son had dared to protest against distortion. 'It will make them respect the boy!' Mamma, more realistic, was less tolerant. 'What would happen if he couldn't go back? Where is a boy without education in Italy today?' She turned sharply to Fabio. 'Do you want to be a road-sweeper? You'd better apologise tomorrow morning and keep out of classes where your sense of justice is affronted.'

But there was no chance to apologise. The headmaster was curt and his ultimatum offered Fabio no opportunity to plead his case. 'Boys come to this school to learn, not to argue. I will not have my teachers insulted.' He rose to his feet and waved briefly towards the door. 'Fabio Santi, you are expelled!'

When he walked into his parents' room, only a little while after he had left it, there was again no opportunity for excuses. For once Mamma lost her self-control and exposed Fabio's classroom courage for the futile piece of folly it really was. Where could a boy get without schooling, even a brilliant boy like Fabio? The university opened the door to any career a man liked to choose, but how could he get to a university after this? They scolded, sobbed and dramatised as only Italians on the edge of calamity can do. This was a situation from which neither piety nor prayer offered any escape.

At the end of what would have been his third year at high school, rather more than a year after his expulsion, Fabio presented himself as a private student for the examinations he would normally have taken at the end of his fourth year at school. If he passed they would qualify him for entrance to the university. He had crowded nearly two year's high school education into one year of private study and passed, a year ahead of his contemporaries, high in the scholarship lists. Very young for the rigorous demands ahead of him, he followed Emanuele and Teofilo to the University of Naples, where he read for a degree in commercial science and economics and gained his doctorate.

His incisive mind and power of speech, however, seemed to fit him for other purposes and, almost inevitably, he re-enrolled as a student in the Faculty of Law and gained his second doctorate. While his brother Teofilo was still working his way through the medical schools Fabio had already set up in legal practice. The disabilities which affected Teofilo's early attempts to gain patients in Portici had no parallel in his own case. No one apparently supposed that a man's religion would affect his legal abilities, and in any case he did not practise in Portici. Instead, he opened an office near where Casa Materna itself had begun thirty years earlier, in the Piazza Nicole Amore. Now the square was busier and the archway where Angelo and Rosetta d'Ambrosio had sold matches was decorated by two carved stone animals. Two or three minutes walk away the apartments in the Via Cimbre, where he had grown up for the first ten years of his life, were occupied by a Waldensian pastor and his family, for Riccardo Santi's church had been handed over by the American Methodists to the Waldensian Church, for centuries the traditional evangelical church in Italy. Even so, the little church was much the same as it had always been, though the congregation had grown larger.

Clients came quickly, though many of them were poor and winning their cases could bring him little profit. At home in Portici, as well as in Naples itself, work poured in, as much because he gave people hope and confidence as because he was a sound lawyer. To Fabio, however, while his legal work was a means of livelihood and winning his cases a satisfaction, Casa Materna was life. Like Teofilo, he never left home. Unlike him, he never married, and the unbounded love he might have given to a wife and family was lavished on the children.

A huge man—in any photograph he seems to tower above everyone round him—he enjoyed every moment of the day. He worked prodigiously hard, both in his office and in the service of the orphanage and the schools, and because his liking for work was matched by a brilliant mind, he got through an incredible amount. His early love of sport continued throughout his life, and his teenage sociability grew into a mature ease in mixing with people of every class. Desperately poor clients from Portici, wealthy families of the town with whom he later mixed in administrative affairs, British and American senior officers of the Allied Governments and of N.A.T.O. found him the same genial, optimistic, far-sighted friend. With so big a frame it was not surprising that he liked good food and good living, or that he spent long hours in the Casa Materna kitchen cooking or devising new dishes for the children from the slender resources of the Santi cupboards. More than any of the family he enjoyed convivial company and social life. Yet, despite his body-shaking laugh, he could be deeply serious. Like Teofilo, he was a lay preacher of the Methodist Church and a member of its Standing Committee and the faith that his father preached so fervently was shown in all he did.

Casa Materna, during the war and in the following fifteen years, probably owed more to him than to any other member of the Santi family.

The family's return from Praiano after the war was a sad homecoming. The pillared villa, their home for twenty years, was in a terrible state of disrepair. The bombing which Naples had suffered and the bombardment which had accompanied the allied advance had left ruin everywhere in the city, and Casa Materna had not escaped. There were shell-holes in the villa, the stables and the house by the road. One of the walls of the villa had collapsed. The garden was not only overgrown with weeds but pitted with craters. Only the big three-storey building by the road was habitable. The villa itself was a repository for stores for the occupying forces. Outside, on the Corso Garibaldi, armoured cars, tanks and lorries rattled along the cobbled road, where the houses on each side bore the same scars as Casa Materna. Every now and again one of the lorries would swing in through the portico and crash through the grounds to the stores, so that Papa and Mamma lived in a perpetual fear that the children would be killed or injured. For the children themselves the first excitement of 'coming home' quickly passed, and there was little fun in sleeping in the barn, on the floor of the big house by the road or in tents provided by the soldiers. In post-war Naples life was disorganised for everyone and the children shared the common tragedy of malnutrition and neurosis. Though, unlike tens of thousands of Neapolitans, they had some sort of accommodation, it was uncertain how long even that security would last. The buildings were still requisitioned by the military authorities and it was not forgotten by Fabio that the high court in 1940 had ruled that the orphanage should be closed as soon as the emergency was over. Italy still had a Government, though it was no longer Fascist, and there might well be those who would try to ensure that the court's ruling was carried out.

Meanwhile, they occupied themselves as busily as they could in repairing the house that might not long be theirs. It was a common sight for the soldiers who came for replenishment of their stores to see the immense figure of Fabio rebuilding one of the villa's walls while a long line of eager children passed the stones up to him. In time, some of the soldiers joined the children in looking for stones and bricks or Fabio in his masonry and bricklaying. With help from allied sources, the Italian Government, the United States and the American Methodist Board of Missions the buildings were put in order within a few years of the family moving back.

Papa was in his middle seventies when the war ended and Mamma about the same age so that Fabio became, in effect, the Director of Casa Materna. Emanuele was still in America, continuing his ministry at Yonkers and doing all he could to stir interest in the work at Portici. Teofilo ran his surgery at Casa Materna and spent a great deal of time dealing with the physical and nervous ailments of the children, but he was deeply involved with social and medical work in Naples and elsewhere. While Fabio's legal work still had to be carried on his main concern was to use every opportunity to enlist support and help for Casa Materna and, in particular, to regain proper control of the property.

Generals, whether American or British, were out of his reach. So were brigadiers. Even the ubiquitous colonels had more than enough to do. 'Top brass' was too concerned with all the tasks involved in sorting out the chaos in which both Fascists and Germans had left the country to spare time for a civilian who wanted to get possession of his home. The war was not over in the West for many months after Fabio began to prepare for the children's return and it was almost a year after that when the Pacific war came to an end with the bombing of Hiroshima. In Naples itself more than half the population was either homeless or existed in shattered or damaged buildings. It is no part of the duties of liberating armies to organise the rebuilding of cities they have devastated. Staff officers were not inhuman but their own duties were onerous enough, while the average soldier, used to the havoc of war, vacillated between compassion which expressed itself in giving away his rations and a tough hard-heartedness because 'these people had asked for it, anyway'. To the American G.I.—and there were far more Americans than British in Naples —the children of Naples made the greatest appeal, despite the fact that many of them had the dishonesty of professional beggars and the practised skill of natural thieves. The only men in the armed services to whom Fabio could quite naturally turn were the chaplains.

His first approach of this kind, as we have seen, was when he gained help for the children and the Praiano villagers who had sheltered them, and the story of Casa Materna was soon widely known. Other chaplains, too, began to take a practical interest. Soon after the children's return to their shattered home in Portici Papa Santi was urged by some of the chaplains to conduct open-air services in Naples itself. This he gladly did, for he was deeply aware of his pastoral responsibilities and had been trying to care for the scattered congregation in Portici from the time the war ended. At Casa Materna itself the chapel was re-opened and from time to time some of the chaplains and the men they served joined the children in worship. Some became regular visitors.

Three chaplains, Moore, Anthony and Zaccara, though they got little encouragement from senior officers, insisted on taking the matter of Casa Materna to General Alexander himself. As a result, Fabio Santi gained more than he had dared to expect. Not only was the full use of the Casa Materna buildings restored but, in addition, permission was given for the re-opening of the schools, which had been closed since Mussolini's edict of 1939.

Immediately, despite the condition of the buildings, Papa and Mamma Santi went into action. Before the war there had been a hundred Portici children in the schools and many of the families remained in the district. The two old people set out from Casa Materna with their faces gayer than they had been for years. They found it hard to restrain themselves from accosting every stranger on the street with the same message.

'God has heard our prayers. We can begin all over again.'

Instead, they went from door to door amongst the families they knew. They spoke to children on the street and sought out those who had once, five or six years earlier, been their pupils.

'The children can come back to school!'

The day after their house-to-house visitation sixty Portici children of all ages turned in through the portal of Casa Materna to join the hundred or more who were already in the orphanage.

The worst was over. Although years of hard work lay ahead before the buildings and equipment were back to standard the tide had begun to run in their favour at last. And during the years of reconstruction Fabio, in spite of his increasing preoccupation with affairs in Portici, was planning for much more than rebuilding. Advance in every area of Casa Materna's life was in his mind.

Practical help came from the men of the 'occupying forces' who found friendship in the Santi home. Methodists, Baptists, Presbyterians, Congregationalists, Lutherans felt themselves at home. If the Methodists, because of the special links with that Church in the United States and because of the plaque on the wall which had touched the young German's heart, had a particular love for this little place of refuge, the organist of the Mormon Temple in Salt Lake City found himself equally happy playing at the service. At the same time, they were appalled by what they saw.

The childrens' clothes were as clean as washing could make them, but laundering had its own dangers. New clothes either for boys or girls had been unobtainable for years and what they had were patched beyond repatching, with all the colour washed out of them. They were barefooted because there was no money for new shoes and in any case they were unobtainable in post-war Naples. The children were shockingly thin, their arms and legs bony and their faces aged and haggard. Despite Teofilo's medical care their skins showed the long lack of vitamins and balanced diet. In all this they were no worse, and indeed considerably better, than most of the tragic children of Naples, but whereas the immensity of the Neapolitan problem was to baffle the Municipality and even U.N.R.R.A. itself, in a small, integrated group like Casa Materna individual kindnesses made all the difference.

The most natural generosity for a soldier to offer was part of his own rations and time after time when they came to worship or to visit the orphanage the G.I.s brought packets of 'hard rations'—their own and all they could collect in their billets.

'Say, *signore* Fabio,' called a soldier who drove in one day, 'I got a truck full of tents here. They ain't no use as tents, though. They been condemned!'

Even Fabio looked surprised. 'I hope we've finished sleeping in tents now we've got the houses back again.'

'You got it wrong, *signore*. They ain't no use to *us*, but I thought mebbe if you was to cut them up they might make better blouses than the ones the girls have got on now!'

'They certainly couldn't make worse ones,' agreed Fabio, and then roared with laughter. 'Though I never imagined I'd see Casa Materna girls dressed in *tents*!'

Nevertheless, the tents *were* made into blouses, and surprisingly good ones, too.

On another occasion it was a sergeant who walked round after service, horrified at the shoeless children. He had come from Florence and conditions in Naples appalled him.

'My name's Clausing, Sergeant Arthur Clausing from Wilmington, California,' he introduced himself to Fabio. 'You've got no money for shoes, I guess?'

'No,' agreed Fabio. 'But have you tried to buy children's shoes in Naples? You just can't get them, sergeant.'

'Could you make them? If I found some leather?'

Fabio laughed, a little grimly. 'There are times when we'd have been glad to *eat* leather. Yes, Sergeant, I fancy we could make some kind of shoes.'

The same afternoon Clausing returned with a truck and began to throw out his 'leather'. Boxing gloves, footballs, old baseball gloves tumbled in a heap on the grass. 'The soldiers haven't got any soles, unfortunately,' he chipped as Fabio sorted through them.

The big man laughed. 'We make soles as well as save them in Casa Materna,' he countered. Make soles they did, though they had to be of wood, and the children were better shod than they had been for many months.

It was not only 'iron rations' that the Army contributed. Chaplain Skoien, whose home was at Chippewa Falls, Wisconsin, was a hospital chaplain and knew something of the difference between Neapolitan food and soldiers' rations. At Casa Materna it was not only such luxuries as shoes that were lacking; often it was food itself. A little often had to go a long way indeed. The chaplain saw how little it was and went back to hospital to talk to his colonel. The result was a truckful of bread and beefsteak, sent with the colonel's compliments—and a new friend for Casa Materna.

A very different kind of gift was made by the Deputy Theatre Chaplain, Dr A. Stanley Trickett. In their search for anything of value the German soldiers had stolen the Communion set from the chapel. Dr Trickett replaced it with one issued for military use. The Theatre Chaplain's association with Casa Materna, however, was much closer than the casual ones which produced blouses and shoes. He was able to gain renewed help from the Methodist Church in the U.S.A. and, somewhat later, when he became Administrator of the Reconstruction Department of the World Council of Churches, his knowledge of Fabio and Teofilo Santi's work gained them invaluable assistance.

On two other notable occasions the U.S. Army chaplains stepped in to achieve what Fabio alone could never have done.

In 1947 came the moment he had been dreading. It transported Fabio, in a moment of anguish, to the day in 1940 when he had waited in Rome for the judgement of the High Court. When it came—that the orphanage should remain open until the end of the war—he said a quiet prayer of thanksgiving. But, even then, he had known it was not the end of the case. Had Italy been victorious, Casa Materna must undoubtedly have been closed. Even when she capitulated it was possible that someone might try to revive the findings of the court. Now, seven years later, the drama was repeated. Orders were issued by the Italian government that the orphanage must be closed.

Fabio discussed the critical situation with a senior chaplain, David L. Ostergren of Albut City, Iowa. This time legal arguments about ownership and complicated case-law, which had prolonged the previous case for month after month, were useless.

'There's just one argument we can put up,' said Ostergren. 'To close Casa Materna is an infringement of religious liberty. And we may have to push that one right through to the top before they'll listen.'

That, indeed, was what Chaplain Ostergren had to do. The case was taken to the supreme allied councils in London, with the backing of American opinion behind it, and the order quashed. By the help of a Lutheran chaplain the house with the open doors was kept open once more.

The second outstanding contribution of the chaplains' department came when Fabio reported that, in order to repair the buildings, he had applied to the Italian Office of Public Works but his application had been turned down. The chaplains' department encouraged him to put in another appeal and ask for an interview. When it was granted they went with him, and the sight of American uniforms brought a new wariness to the office. Fabio presented his case once more. The chaplains represented that this was not a denominational organisation. It refused no children on religious grounds. All children in need were accepted, so far as funds permitted. Just as much as any other rehabilitation work in Naples it was a piece of social service and as such deserved help. In the end Fabio was granted funds to repair the 'war damage' to the villa, and before the military occupation ended he had received 16,000,000 lire for its complete restoration.

Slowly conditions began to improve, through the compassion of those who had briefly been the enemies of Italy. Church World Service sent from America such things as cereals, soup, macaroni. Vitamins and drugs came, too, and with Teofilo's guidance were put to the best use. There were even occasions when, because a shipment of white flour had arrived at the port, the children had white bread to eat, though these times were rare indeed.

The years of war receded. By the early 1950s there were children in the school to whom the war was not even a memory. In the orphanage itself, on the other hand, many of the older children remembered it only too vividly. Some were there because parents had been killed in the bombardment or because fathers had died in battle. Others were not Italian children at all, but had been transferred from the refugee camps where Teofilo was at work, and long after the city of Naples had begun to assume something of its post-war gaiety the camps continued to send these sad-faced waifs to be cared for by the Santis.

Though Fabio's activities outside Casa Materna, and some of his work in the orphanage itself, can be more conveniently followed in the next chapter it will be helpful to see at this point how some of his dreams began to take shape. Some five years after the war ended the first new building was begun and with it one of Teofilo's visions came true. It was a small sanatorium, since enlarged, near the main villa.

Nine years after their return from Praiano a great new concrete block was built on the opposite side of the villa from the infirmary, and Casa Materna's crowded schoolchildren had a new and worthy place of their own. The School Building owed its existence, in the main, to the generosity of American Methodism which contributed 100,000 dollars towards its erection.

Four years later, in 1957, another large block was opened as a dormitory and living-accommodation for the older boys, but while this too owed a good deal to American help it was also the result of Fabio's own initiative, as the next chapter will explain.

Because 'high school education' is less useful to many Italian boys than more practical courses, technical education was more fully provided for as the years went by. In 1954 the carpentry shop was opened. This was followed in 1961 by a radio and television repair shop, largely equipped by United States 'Eagles'. The sanatorium had already been enlarged by the generosity of a Swiss lady. In 1962 the machine-shop for the training of mechanics who would later be apprenticed in industry was opened in the old stables by the farmhouse, and its equipment was partly provided by the American organisation, CARE.

In the same way as boys were fitted for later life by basic training suited to their own abilities, so girls were equipped for the more ordinary positions open to them. Particular attention was given to domestic science, sewing, dressmaking and embroidery for those who were not likely to get full value from a 'grammar school' education. More lately commercial subjects—typewriting, shorthand and secretarial courses—have been introduced.

All who could do so have been encouraged to go on to grammar-school subjects, and from this group, throughout its existence, have come teachers, nurses, ministers, doctors and university graduates in ever-increasing numbers.

The tiny kindergarten which Ersilia Santi started in their overcrowded apartments in the Piazza della Borsa has grown into a school of some 400 or more children, well-housed, adequately staffed and adapted to contemporary needs. To the Santis its basis has always been religious, a point well illustrated by the visit of a government school inspector. The inspector was greatly impressed by all he saw and clearly prepared to write a very good report—until he noticed one omission as he visited a class-room. He went back and looked in the others, growing more angry as he did so.

'You have no crucifix in any of your class-rooms,' he shouted.
'No. We are Protestants.'
'If you have no crucifix you must be Communists!'

Still protesting, he was led to the entrance hall and shown a picture which hung there, a picture of Jesus welcoming the children and blessing them.

'*That* stands here instead of a crucifix. It is the symbol of all we do and the reason why we do it.'

10

Death on the Road to Rome

THE year was 1950.

Fabio's bedroom was on the ground-floor of the villa, and from the window he could see Naples on his right and, to the left, the Sorrento peninsula and Capri. In the light of early morning—and Fabio always rose early—the view was ethereal. At night the lights seemed to dance in the distance as the liners, fully illuminated, moved out of the port. Watching them go he felt his heart drawn with them, towards America and towards Emanuele. How good it would be if he would come home!

Not that Emanuele was unwilling to come. It was his friends and his bishop who dissuaded him with what seemed unassailable logic. 'You're much more useful where you are. Does it really take three brilliant men to run an orphanage?' 'Three men in Naples!' thought Fabio. Papa Santi was already eighty. Mamma, still clear in mind and sharp of voice, was feeling the pangs of arthritis so that it was a struggle, sometimes, even with a stick, to climb the marble staircase to their apartments in the long roadside building. Teofilo, now married and living in the same house, was occupied with new work in Naples. Three men too many in Naples! Fabio was drawn away from the window, from his thoughts, by a knock on the door.

It might be a teacher with a classroom problem ... a child to ask advice from Uncle Fabio about his future ... a shabby man or woman for Fabio the lawyer ... Teofilo, to plunge without introduction into some new aspect of his work in the slums ... one or other was always at the door. Today it was a friend, complaining that the Communists had controlled the local Council long enough and it was time the Liberals came to power, which they certainly would if the right man led them. For the Director of Casa Materna, still busy as a lawyer, there was always too much to do.

Yet it was just at this point, in his late thirties and when the immediate demands and future plans for Casa Materna seemed to be taxing him to the utmost, that Fabio heard a call from God.

He decided to enter politics.

It seemed a strange decision. Only twenty years earlier, when he was at the university, Protestants and Liberals were anathema to Portici and the Santis themselves objects of suspicion. But during those twenty years, and especially since the war, many things had changed. Portici itself had grown rapidly in size and population as people had moved out from the centre of Naples during the bombardment or sought less damaged homes there when it was over. The result had been terrible overcrowding in the courts and tenements but also an explosion of new ideas amongst them. With the overthrow of the Fascists the Communists came into the open and gained the public support of those who had given the guerilla groups surreptitious approval in more dangerous days. This support was clearly shown in the elections when town after town, including Portici, came under Communist control.

To many Italians Fascism and Catholicism were linked together and the Communists made effective use of the Church's official support of Mussolini. But while one result was a more stubborn resistance of the right-wing parties to the attack on their religious and political principles a more unexpected one was a growing support amongst Catholics for the middle-of-the-road Liberal party, for almost a century the natural home of the Evangelicals. Thoughtful Catholics envisaged more hope under a Liberal Government than they had known under Fascism and certainly more than they would find under doctrinaire Communism.

Fabio had all the qualities likely to make him popular in elections for the local council. He had the gift of oratory and had spent himself in the service of the poor. Many families, unable to pay the most meagre fee, had come to him because their case seemed hopeless and been cheered by his friendly assurance that 'there *must* be some way through'. He was popular with his professional colleagues, while his interest in sport gave him a standing with ordinary people. More important, the Santi family, after much tribulation, had achieved a unique position in Portici and were both respected and loved. But to Fabio the one thing that mattered was his conviction that God needed him in the political world. Only by involvement could a Christian in the modern world do anything to change society into something more like the Kingdom of God.

He allowed his name to go forward as a Liberal candidate and was elected with a majority that astonished him. The result was even more significant than it seemed. Fabio was the first Protestant ever to be elected to the Council in Portici.

To the Liberals his election brought new hope. They needed a leader and Fabio was their unanimous choice. The year after he was returned he challenged the ruling Communist party again at the elections and led the Liberals to power in a sweeping victory. Amongst the Catholics the right wing opposed them but it was Catholic support that took them to the Municipality. For many of the priests Fabio's candidature posed a personal problem and there were not a few who stood uneasily by the conservative party line in public but who counselled their parishioners in private to vote for 'Fabio, the honest man'.

'Fabio for Mayor!'

The cry, common in the streets, was echoed in the council chamber immediately after the Liberal victory. It illustrates more than the general approval of a good man. To those who worked with him he was never 'Dr Santi'; always 'Fabio'. Even now, nearly ten years after his last appearance in the council chamber, his successors in the municipal administration still talk of 'Fabio's road', 'Fabio's hospital'; still say 'Fabio would have done this' or 'Fabio would not have agreed to that'. He not only broke down the enmity of those who disagreed with him; he seemed to give an immediate assurance to those who worked with him, as he did to the children and the poor, that he was an intimate friend.

Accepting the mayoralty, however, involved serious difficulties. In a Catholic township the mayor must attend Catholic churches and share in Catholic ceremonies and this, in conscience, he could not do. The dilemma was quickly solved by the council. They appointed an older man to represent him on such occasions while they gave Fabio their full approval for refusing to compromise his conscience.

Fabio now found himself with three offices—one in Naples, in the Piazza della Borsa; another in Casa Materna, which was never free of the sound of children's voices; a third, the mayor's parlour itself, in the Municipal building not far from St Ciro's cathedral in the *piazza*. The mayor's office soon seemed likely to be busiest of the three. What some men might have accepted as an honour with a number of official obligations Fabio immediately began to use an opportunity for an immense amount of public service. In the years that followed he almost wore out everybody but himself. His energy was prodigious and matched his broad vision for the town he loved. As in Casa Materna itself, he could not be satisfied with things as they were. It was always his mood that 'there was so much to be done' and it seems as if some deep awareness of the future drove him to do as much as he could while there was still time. Like all the Santis he was interested in education. Just as naturally he was concerned about medical facilities, gravely inadequate in the growing town. Yet, because he was far-sighted, he refused to make these obvious areas of reform his chief concern.

'Our real problem is housing,' he declared. His fellow-councillors nodded their agreement. 'We are in danger of producing more slums than we already have. People keeping trying to move in, but they aren't all the kind of people we need. We want more office-workers, more people engaged in administration and the professions if Portici is to become the sort of town we dream of!'

Some of his friends were not dreaming of any sort of town at all. All they hoped for was to reform the administration of the one they already had. 'How can we expect such people to move into Portici?' they shrugged.

'We can't. We must build the sort of apartments they will want to use.'

'But there's no room for that kind of building.'

'Then,' replied Fabio, 'we must pull down what we have—and build better houses in its place.'

Immediately there was uproar in the chamber. The conservatives protested about destroying the town as it was. The left-wing members shouted in defence of those whose homes would be destroyed. Even Fabio's supporters questioned the possibility of gaining the necessary ministerial sanction.

'Where would you build such houses?'

'On a main thoroughfare leading from this central *piazza* out to the Pompeii road.'

The councillors gaped at him. 'But there is no such road.'

'Exactly!' agreed Fabio. 'So we can begin from the very beginning. We can make a road . . . a road a mile long, perhaps . . . a road lined with good shops and fine apartments . . . a road that will change the whole character of Portici.' Before they could interrupt he slapped his big hand down on the table before him and caught up a sheaf of drawings. 'Look!' He thrust them towards the startled members. 'This is what I have in mind. See these plans? . . . here is the *piazza* . . . the municipality . . . now, through these tenements beyond the cathedral where I have drawn a red line. . . .'

As Fabio talked they began to see a new vision . . . a new road with clean, tall houses on each side, brightened by coloured shutters . . . well-dressed men and women in the attractive shops. . . .

'We must call it Via Fabio Santi!' shouted one member.

'You can't call a road after a man until he's been dead for ten years,' countered another. 'And Fabio's very much alive just now!'

Today that road runs precisely where Fabio first planned it. The *Via Liberta* is straight, wide, attractive. It did all he hoped for, and changed not only the face but the character of Portici. Old tenements were swept away, though there was a great deal of difficult negotiation before that was done. New people sought the new apartments, as well as those who had lost their homes. The population of the town, beginning to rise when the war ended, leapt from its pre-war figure of 18,000 to 60,000.

Without this plan, which dominated the discussions of the Municipality for months but was turned into reality with astonishing speed, Fabio's other schemes would have had less chance of success. New property meant new taxes in the municipal treasury; new people meant more money in circulation. They also implied more children to be educated and more sick folk needing aid.

In Italy, education is compulsory—on the statute book. In fact, there are villages with no schools, many towns with too few. Because of the lack of space children attend state schools either morning or afternoon but not both. On the other hand, if sufficient buildings were available for full-day education there would not be enough teachers to staff the schools.

'Portici needs a teacher-training college,' the mayor asserted. 'But,' he went on before anyone could argue, 'it's no use delaying training teachers until we have a college to do it in.'

'There's no building big enough.'

'We can start in a small way. Here in the town hall!'

There were immediate protests from the officials. Their offices were already too small. 'You know that, Fabio! You're here every day. Where is there an office that could be used?'

'Perhaps you could train teachers in the mayor's parlour?'

There was an appreciative laugh round the table, which died away as Fabio answered. 'No—we can hardly do that. But if we move some of the clerks . . .' he enumerated half a dozen '. . . *they* can bring their desks in my office and that will leave a room free for us to begin training. There won't be many at the beginning. By the time we overflow from here we must have other plans in mind.'

Teachers are being trained in Portici now, though the days of the crowded mayor's office are long past.

The third scheme on which Fabio set his mind was a municipal hospital and he saw clearly where he wanted it, near the new *Via Liberta*. Not even with himself in control of the council could everything be achieved at once. The hospital is not yet built. But that the plans, many of them with his own notes and modifications on them, will become a reality before long is certain.

All the time he was helping to transform Portici, Fabio was planning for the more effective growth of Casa Materna, and the new buildings in the lovely compound matched the growth of the town itself. Neither Papa nor Mamma Santi ever realised how gently the responsibility had been eased from their old shoulders —by Livia, Teofilo's wife, now becoming an effective partner in the administration; by Teofilo who gave more time than he could properly spare from his other commitments and above all by Fabio. He needed all the additional help he could find. It was with some eagerness, therefore, that he read a letter from Emanuele, then still ministering at Yonkers.

'*I have a young man here, Joel Warner, who is wondering if he could give some temporary service at Casa Materna. . . .*'

It was an offer which was to have surprising results.

Joel Warner's father was a Methodist minister of the New York

Conference but Joel, like Emanuele, had no intention of following the same profession. The trouble, however, was that this was only one of a number of things he did not want to be, a condition made worse by the fact that there did not seem to be anything he *did* want to do—not even to cultivate the musical gifts he had inherited from his mother. Mrs Warner was a singer, and she had met Luisa Santi when they were both at Columbia University in the early 1920s. Luisa had encouraged her with stories of Naples and those who had begun their careers at the Opera House there and when Luisa returned to Portici her friend came too. She did indeed sing at the Teatro San Carlo, and though she sacrificed her musical career to marry a Methodist minister her friendship with Luisa continued, and was the basis of the family's interest in Emanuele. It was Emanuele who had suggested that a spell at Casa Materna might help to mature Joel's character and give him time to think clearly about his future. Joel had very readily agreed.

Fabio, who accepted him readily enough, became increasingly uncertain that it was a good idea after all. Joel arrived in the early part of 1955, but after the first few weeks he still seemed restless and unsettled. His knowledge of Italian was rudimentary and he did not seem anxious to learn more than he had to for everyday purposes. He looked in at classes; ate his communal meals with the children; watched the girls at their embroidery, the boys at their carpentry and the smaller children at their games—yet his mood was devoid of enthusiasm. Teofilo and Fabio watched him with deepening frustration. He was likeable, but something of a liability. After a while they gave up any attempt to fit him in, and waited.

The problem was resolved when they gave up trying. One afternoon Fabio went into the music room and found Joel surrounded by a group of boys and girls—singing.

'You seem to have a gift for bringing the music out of them,' Fabio said to him later.

'They have some fine voices,' commented Joel. 'I might try and make some of them into a choir. If you agree, of course.' It was his first sign of enthusiasm.

Fabio was delighted. Music, always an integral part of Casa Materna life, might well be of more specific use. If there were a choir they could give concerts. . . .

The children responded to Joel as they had done to no one else and from this untrained material he produced a choir fit to sing far beyond the halls of the orphanage. Then, as it seemed out of nowhere, came the great idea.

'Why shouldn't we go on tour?'

'Where?' asked Teofilo.

Fabio's audacity left them speechless. 'The United States!'

Of course it was impossible. Even Joel realised the absurdity of the idea—until Emanuele came on holiday to Portici that same year. Money was needed to take the children to America? He could surely raise it for a special project of this kind. An itinerary would have to be prepared? With help he could do that, too. Publicity was essential, preferably undertaken by someone who really knew Casa Materna at first-hand? Joel Warner could return to the States with him at the end of his holiday and deal with it. The impossible began to become reality.

During the rest of the year Fabio gave endless time, more than he could properly afford, to training the children. A repertoire was carefully prepared, including operatic choruses ranging from *Traviata* to *Aida*. New teachers were engaged to teach the children English so that they could sing British and American songs. French and German songs were added. In particular, a wide range of traditional Neapolitan music was drawn on since this was what a foreign audience would expect to hear and enjoy. By the end of 1955 arrangements on the Italian side were complete.

In America, too, affairs were well in hand. Joel was showing great gifts as an organiser and publicist. For a tour which was to last five months the most detailed planning was essential and Emanuele had it well in hand. The cost could not be less than 12,000 dollars and might be more. Sponsors were needed. Homes must be found for the children in each town where they would be performing—and hosts must be warned that big Italian boys liked big plates of spaghetti!

In January, 1956, thirty-four boys and girls set sail for the United States with Fabio on the *Cristofero Colombo*.

To Fabio the moment as they steamed out of the bay was one for thankfulness—but it held other implications. The municipal elections were due while he was away and the tour involved the temporary renunciation of his political life. To concentrate on preparing for it, he had already had to relinquish his mayoral office.

It would be easy to write a whole chapter describing the tour and the children's adventures on it. From the moment they finished their brief fits of weeping as the mainland faded out of sight the whole six months were a triumph. Fabio enjoyed every moment of it, until almost the very end. His geniality won him new friends wherever he went. The reunions with Emanuele and Luisa and her husband and children were worth the whole journey. The enthusiasm of the audiences and the excitement of the choir were boundless. Yet, at the same time, his prayers for the family at home were strangely urgent. They seemed so far away—he could understand now how Emanuele had always felt and especially during the war when the separation was so complete. Papa had seemed so old and Mamma so frail as he had embraced them before he left. Teofilo was there, of course, and Livia, but for the first time more of the family was away than at home.

The first engagements when they landed in America were to make a recording for R.C.A. and to appear on radio and television programmes. Then, on February 20th, at Scarsdale Congregational Church, New York, the tour began. Originally it had been intended that they should give three or four concerts a week, but their reputation grew so quickly that the schedule was immediately enlarged. On their first twenty days they gave twenty-two official concerts, and in their tour they travelled throughout the whole country. They had their own coach, and no one could have been more helpful than the driver. Fabio and Joel went with them everywhere. In five months they had over 110 concerts in churches, schools, clubs and so on. They sang in 34 states, as widely separated as New York, Ohio and Virginia, Connecticut, California and Texas.

In each concert they sang the first half in formal dress and the second half in Italian national costume. In the interval Fabio, huge amongst the children, addressed the audience and told them something of Casa Materna. The 'notices' were uniformly excellent. They were compared with the 'Vienna Boys' Choir' and collected two large books of 'cuttings'. Money came in generously, and the new boys' block which Fabio hoped to build as a result of the tour became more of a possibility as each day passed. Fabio was as happy with the Americans as they were with him.

If anyone was happier than Fabio himself it was Joel Warner, but this was not merely because the tour owed so much to his initiative or even because his personal problems were solved and he could now see the way ahead. The leading soprano of the choir was a charming girl from the Italian hill-country, Ida Mastri. To Joel, the sun shone all day because he had fallen in love.

Then came tragedy.

When the choir was almost at the end of its triumphant tour Luisa had a cable from Teofilo in Naples. She shared the news immediately with Emanuele. Ersilia Santi, Mamma the beloved, was dead.

They debated about telling Fabio, who was perhaps closer to his mother than any of the rest of the family, and decided against it, keeping the news from him for a while, but it could not be done for long. The press were bound to hear of it and, with the choir in America, it was certain to be bracketed with the news of their tour. Luisa flew back to Italy to be there in time for the funeral and Fabio was left to comfort the stricken children as best he could in the midst of his own grief.

The tour ended and on 7th July, 1956, the choir boarded the *Conte Biancamano* for the journey home. The last programme was recorded aboard ship for the 'Voice of America' and the children sang 'America the beautiful' as they drew away from shore. For thirteen days they revelled in the freedom of the whole ship, granted to them by the Captain, Commandante Giovanni Sandri, and gave concerts in the first and second class lounge.

Fabio sat in his cabin to write a message of gratitude to their American friends.

'.... *We shall never forget the majesty of your country, the beauty of your communities, but above all else we shall remember your kindness and unequalled hospitality. We travelled many miles and met many people, yet we were never among strangers. .... From the immediate results of the tour we are now in a financial position to begin construction of the new dormitory for older boys. ....*'

He put his pen down and thought back over the tour. There were so many things he must tell Teofilo, Livia, Papa. So many things he would have wanted especially to share with Mamma. Even now he could hardly bear to think of their loss.

After calling at Lisbon, Barcelona, Genoa and Palermo the ship drew in to the port of Naples. Hundreds of friends were gathered to welcome them home, and in the middle of the crowd was the Casa Materna band. Representatives of Italian radio and television were there to describe their homecoming and a programme was recorded for all-Italian transmission.

Only one person was missing, and the last song of the choir's tour was sung at Mamma Santi's grave.

The choir, however, had another very special engagement before the next year was finished.

Joel Warner returned to Naples to organise publicity for the orphanage and to work out a correspondence link with those who had become firm friends with many members of the choir. Out of this was born the *Casa Materna News*, which may still be obtained by all who are interested in the work at Portici. But Joel had another more personal reason for returning.

In June 1957 he and Ida Mastri were married at Ida's mountain village, Neofoggia, where her parents were staunch members of a tiny Salvation Army corps. The Casa Materna choir went to sing at the wedding. Later that same year Joel returned to America to enrol in the Theological School of Yale University. His wife, Ida, opened a kindergarten school and busied herself with social work until he had finished training for the ministry and they went to their first pastorate at Port Washington.

Though Fabio's homecoming was distressing because of the tragedy at Casa Materna there was another aspect of it which uplifted him.

Because of preparations for the tour and his being away for six months his political life had had to be put aside. Despite this, his name had been put forward once more as a Liberal candidate. With no opportunity for canvassing or speeches he would not have been surprised had he failed to retain his seat. Instead, to his astonishment, he was returned to the Municipality with an overwhelming majority, and his name was at the top of the poll.

Teofilo, to whom his brother was the greatest man in Naples, exulted in the result. Plans which Fabio had only begun to put into action would be fulfilled and new ones conceived. The boys' dormitory would be only one of a series of new schemes for the extension of education in Casa Materna. True, there were moments when Fabio said, with an unusual wistfulness, that he would not live to see all his hopes come true—but every man of vision feels that same frustration of time's swift passing. It might be that Teofilo would have to curtail some of his medical practise to give Fabio more time for his political life, but he was beginning to feel that this was inevitable, in any case.

Portici was a different town now. Not merely in buildings and the new road but in atmosphere. Teofilo, with customary humility, paid tribute to Fabio as the main cause of this, but he himself had had a great part in bringing it about. Together these two brothers, doctor and lawyer, living out the true Christian's commitment to the community, had built bridges between Catholic and Protestant that no amount of preaching or theological discussion could ever do. Both of them were respected and beloved. To Teofilo, after Fabio's tremendous success in the elections, it was clear that his brother was destined for far greater responsibilities than the mayoralty of Portici. Almost certainly he must become a deputy in the Italian Parliament at Rome.

On 23rd October, 1956, Fabio had an appointment in Rome, at the Standing Committee of the Methodist Church, to be followed by a meeting of the National Christian Council. The previous night, he stayed up late clearing his desk of papers and writing to Emanuele. Once more he renewed the plea he had made in America. Would he not come back to Naples? The following morning, after rising early with only a few hours in bed, he spent on municipal business and interviewing people before leaving for Rome. As he came into the house Teofilo teased him about the flowers in his arms.

'An assignation in Rome, eh?'

Fabio smiled gently. 'They are for Mamma's grave. I will go up to the cemetery before I go into Naples.' He waved as he left the room. '*Arrivederci*, Teofilo. I'll pick up Pastor Incelli after I've been with these.'

October can be very hot on the *autostrada*. Naples to Rome is not a long journey; just over 130 miles. Halfway there Fabio and Incelli, the Methodist pastor from Naples, stopped for a meal washed down with some country wine.

'You wouldn't like to sleep before we go on?'

Pastor Incelli shrugged. 'It's only sixty miles or so. Nothing at all to this new Fiat "600" of yours. We'll sleep better in a bed in Rome.'

Fabio let in the clutch and the car shot forward towards Rome. The tedious miles of the *autostrada* clicked by on the speedometer as they drove through the hot afternoon.

Later that evening an officer of the *carbinieri* rang the bell at Teofilo's flat. The doctor was at home and opened the door.

'I'm afraid it's bad news, *signore*.' The man was clearly distressed. 'Dr Fabio Santi has had an accident on the way to Rome. He is badly injured and in hospital. You should go at once, please.'

The doctor stared at him, tried to answer and went back into the flat. It was only four months since Mamma's death; and now this. 'There's been an accident,' he said. Then he added: 'I think Fabio is dead'.

What had happened nobody really knows. The road was clear and undoubtedly Fabio was driving fast. The mechanism of the car did not seem to have failed and it is most likely that, in the heat, he fell asleep. The car swung across the empty road and crashed against a post on the far side. Fabio died instantly, impaled on the steering column. Pastor Incelli was knocked unconscious and never even remembered the accident.

In Rome, hardly knowing how he got there, Teofilo could not face identifying the body and merely waited, unable to think or feel anything, to accompany it back to Naples.

The Italians behave as though death is as important as life. They make no pretence of hiding their sorrow, and a hearse is more magnificent than a wedding carriage. Grief belongs to the community as well as the family. Yet, knowing all this, even the stricken Teofilo was not prepared for what followed.

In Rome he had been comforted by his Methodist friends, and arrangements had been made that they, too, should travel back to Naples with the hearse. It was a slow, sad journey. The Reverend Emanuele Sbaffi, leader of Italian Methodism, and Reginald Kissack, an ex-army chaplain who had returned to Italy as minister of the English Methodist Church in Rome, travelled with Teofilo. Almost all their talk was of Fabio, but they spoke, too, of Papa Santi, stricken twice in less than a year, waiting at the other end, and of the children to whom there could never be anyone like Uncle Fabio again. If they thought of their homecoming it was in terms of a quiet and sorrowful entry into the quiet gardens of Casa Materna.

Then, on the outskirts of Naples, the hearse stopped. Traffic had been halted in Naples. Waiting at the roadside was the Prefect of Naples, hat in hand and head bowed. Behind him stood the Parliamentary deputies for the city and the members of the Naples City Council. They brought messages of sympathy for the family and a request from the Mayor of Partici that the body should lie in state at the Municipality.

Overcome by this reception Teofilo could hardly speak. 'Fabio would want to be at Casa Materna,' he said. 'Thank the mayor, please. He knew Fabio. He will understand.'

The cortège moved on into Naples and through the city, now no longer a sad little procession but one touched with dignity as the Prefect and the great men of the city accompanied it to Portici. Teofilo looked at the streets and wept again. For Fabio's homecoming they were thronged with still crowds. Led by the Prefect the cortège turned from the silent road into the grounds of Casa Materna. From the roof of the villa, over the pillared entrance, came children's voices, singing. It was the choir, singing the same hymns they had sung six months earlier with Fabio in the United States. They sang as the gardens filled with people from the street and the coffin was carried into the Assembly Hall of the school, and then broke off to give way to their desperate grief.

By request there were to be no flowers but, long before the service began at 2.0 o'clock the following day, the balcony was piled high with them. The School Assembly Hall was thronged and crowds who were unable to get in stood in silence outside. The high and certain notes of the Evangelical faith were heard in hymns, the prayers, the scriptures, the sermon. Fabio had been a man of the people, who had loved his family, his friends, his children and hundreds of others. But more than this he was a man of God who had loved God and served Him with all his powers. Those who heard and shared in the service were undeterred by ecclesiastical barriers. Catholic and Protestant thanked God together for Fabio Santi.

Reginald Kissack, in fluent Italian, paid tribute to his friend.

Emanuele Sbaffi preached the sermon, a fervent declaration of God's grace and goodness. Yet though it was a very long service the passage of the cortège to the cemetery was longer still. The streets were closed to traffic, and massed with people, men in sober clothes, women in black, and everywhere they wept. The procession moved very slowly through the crowds.

Now, however, all had passed out of the hands of the family. The Municipality had taken over. The whole massive procession was marshalled by the heralds.

The Prefect of Naples was in his official robes. The parliamentary deputies who had met the hearse on the previous day were swelled by the whole administration. Lawyers and university professors came behind them. The children of Casa Materna walked silently, together with the two hundred and fifty children of the Casa Materna schools. The members of the Portici Council waited to join the cortège in the *piazza*, where it came to a halt. On the balcony of the Municipality the mayor delivered the official oration. It was by his order, he announced, that the procession would take the longer way to the cemetery. No other way would be fitting. It must go by 'Fabio's road'.

It is perhaps two miles or so to the cemetery of Portici from the gates of Casa Materna, but it was not until 7.0 o'clock in the evening that the procession reached it.

Riccardo Santi stood by the grave, where he had taken the service for his wife in the summer, to speak again the words of committal he had so often spoken as a Methodist minister. His voice never faltered. At the age of 87 he saw death as a gate that opened immediately into a new life with the Lord whom Ersilia and Fabio had loved.

Slowly the crowds dispersed.

'Never was such a funeral known in Portici,' wrote a reporter. He added another comment. 'All this for a Protestant!' Then he echoed the cry of the processional marshals. 'All this for Fabio Santi!'

11

Emanuele Comes Home

DR EMANUELE SANTI, after some thirty years in the United States, was a man of some distinction. Not only was he well-known as a musician and minister but his connection with the Casa Materna Society and his share in organising the choir's tour had put him into touch with a very wide church public. In the autumn of 1956 he was the guest preacher at one of the Methodist Conferences.

It was while he was carrying out this duty that news was given to him of his brother Fabio's tragic death on the road to Rome. Since he could not do so himself, Luisa flew back to Italy immediately, leaving her husband far from well at home. Emanuele knew only such details as she had been able to give him and it was an added shock when, a few days later, he received a letter addressed in Fabio's own writing. It was the last letter Fabio had written the night before he died.

'Come back home, Emanuele.' Fabio was renewing his old plea. 'Think of what the three of us could do together!'

Emanuele dropped the thin paper on his desk. There could never be three of them now. At Portici, indeed, there was now only Teofilo, apart from Papa, and he could imagine Teofilo's grief, for he and Fabio had been linked in an intimacy of experience ever since they were children, living, working, planning and worshipping together throughout their lives. After forty-five years of brotherly comradeship Teofilo might well find the tragedy almost unendurable, and in any case he had too many commitments already . . . his medical practice . . . his work at Casa Mia . . . the plans for the hospital in which Fabio too had been so closely involved. . . .

For Emanuele the moment of decision had fully come. He went to see his superior in the New York Conference, Bishop Newell.

'You can do more good here than in Naples!' The old argument, often effective, was now no more than a tentative piece of persuasion. 'You've done well here, Emanuele. We shall miss you if you go.' The bishop was reluctant, even now, to give way. 'But we know your heart is in Naples. We'll see what we can do. Talk it over with your church.'

Then came a letter from Teofilo. 'We need all the money you can raise in America, Emanuele. But we need *you* more!'

The church on White Plains pressed the other argument.

'We'll raise your salary if that will help you.' Emanuele refused gently. 'We'll raise more money for Casa Materna.' In other days that might have been almost decisive, but not now. 'We really need your leadership here at White Plains.' But how desperately short of leadership was the Evangelical Church in Italy.

By Christmas they knew it was no use persuading him further, but even then, when he announced after the Christmas services that he would be leaving early in the New Year there was genuine distress at the news. His car and furniture were sold and he prepared to leave, though his discharge was by no means complete. He was to remain a minister of the Methodist Church in the United States, but would be permitted to serve, without salary or allowances, as Director of Casa Materna. Nothing could have suited the situation better. The close link between Italy and the Church by whose generosity Casa Materna was built up and the villa at Portici secured would be firmer than ever. Still, today, Emanuele Santi is an American Methodist minister and an American citizen.

Towards the middle of January, 1957, he sailed for Italy on the *Cristofero Colombo*, the ship on which the choir had travelled to the United States with Fabio only a year before.

It was some six months or so later that Joel Warner, with his bride Ida, returned to the States not only to extend the support for Casa Materna but to enter the Methodist ministry. In doing so he was carrying out one of the last things Fabio had urged him to do.

Back in Naples, only eighteen months after he had been on holiday there, Emanuele found the atmosphere of Casa Materna subdued and sad. The children were still shadowed by 'Uncle Fabio's' death and perhaps nothing could have done the home more good than the arrival of 'Uncle Emanuele', already much beloved, to take his place.

Teofilo, too, was not the man Emanuele had last seen. He had lost much of his verve and enthusiasm. The distress had cut deeply and it would be a long time before the wound of that October day would heal. But at least he was about his business again, involved in the affairs of his settlement house in Naples and his plans for the new hospital. The Christmas celebrations for the children had forced him into activity he would rather have avoided. Only after he had talked with those who had been at Portici during the previous two months did Emanuele realise how desperately he had been needed.

Hulda Stettler, an American woman who had become Teofilo's colleague in his other work in the Neapolitan slums, talked of what had happened during those months ... of how the calendar had stood at the date of Fabio's death ... of the sack with the broken remains of the steering-wheel which had lain in a corner of Fabio's room ... of how for weeks Teofilo refused even to attend the staff meetings at the slum settlement ... and of the way in which, finally, she and one of his doctor colleagues had thrust in on his grief, turned the calendar, taken away the broken remains of the car and almost forced him back into life. That Fabio should have died was tragic enough; that Teofilo should still be so benumbed and nerveless was perhaps worse still.

Yet Fabio's loss was not, of course, the only one. Mamma had died only a few months earlier, though to those who knew the intimacy that lay between herself and her youngest son this seemed more mercy than sorrow. Now, adding to the tragic year, Luisa received word that her husband was suffering from an incurable disease and was likely to live only a short while. She must return to America at once.

From those who had been there Emanuele heard of Mamma's last months. There had been several months of illness, during which she was confined to bed, a frustrating experience for one who had been so active but one which she took with astonishing calmness. For the last day or so of her life she had known she was dying. At the end she repeated *The Lord is my shepherd*, always her favourite psalm. Then, quite confidently and happily, she spoke again.

'I am going to my beautiful home.'

A few moments later she seemed to go to sleep, and breathed no more.

Mamma's passing was certainly the death of a great woman but to Casa Materna it was much more. Though, like most Italian women of her time, she had taken little part in public life, for fifty-two years, since the day she accepted Angelo and Rosetta into her husband's frugal birthday-party, she had been the master-builder of all that Casa Materna had become. She shared Riccardo Santi's love for the children and her faith in God was as unshakeable as his own. Yet, at the same time, she seldom allowed her heart to rule her head. If her husband's dreams came true, it was largely because she herself refused to dream. If God gave them money in the most unexpected ways, it was put to the best possible use because she held the purse-strings. Without Riccardo's deep compassion Casa Materna would never have begun; but without Ersilia's practical and sometimes astringent common-sense it would have become a chaotic and slightly crazy venture in doing good, doomed to the failure which is the end of so much impractical idealism. Apart from her faith, on which her whole life was based, Ersilia Santi's outstanding quality was her practicality. She immersed herself in work. Her qualities were complementary to Riccardo's, while their concerns —for the Church, for children and education—were mutual. She matched his affection for the children with a strong but never unjust discipline and countered his sunny optimism that God would always provide with a realistic assessment of how far God wanted them to be committed at any one time.

Her organising ability was immense, and she ran the kitchens, the dining-room and the school in pre-war Casa Materna at Portici with the same competence as she had their first flat in the Piazza della Borsa. Her voice was hard, almost strident; wherever the children were, they heard and obeyed. One of her outstanding gifts was a phenomenal memory. She knew the names of all the children in the home and not only what they were supposed to be doing at any particular time but what they actually were doing; there were times when they felt she could see through the walls. It was more surprising that she knew the names, backgrounds, stories and records of almost every child who had passed through

Casa Materna. Not only so, she knew, as though she carried their case-histories about with her, what they had been doing since they left.

Her two special contributions to the development of Casa Materna were in the realms of education and music. From her first kindergarten she tried to offer the best education available, and her family's contributions in this field undoubtedly derived from her own interest in it. Music she had loved from her earliest days, and until her arthritic hands could no longer deal with the keys she continued to play at the services in the Casa Materna chapel.

But her interests were far wider than the school and the home; wider, indeed, one suspects, than her husband's. To the end of her life she enjoyed radio concerts, listening to music and orchestras she would not otherwise have heard. By the same means she was able to keep abreast of world events. She knew what was going on, and formed her own sharp judgements about international affairs. It was probably from her that Fabio, emotionally so tied to her, derived his passion for politics as a practical expression of Christian faith.

At the end of her life she could walk only with a stick. At 6.30 precisely each morning came the tap of her stick on the marble bedroom floor as she moved from her bed to the bathroom. From that moment the day was filled until she went to bed at night. Indeed, it could properly be said that no one lived a fuller life than Ersilia Santi, despite the fact that for fifty-five years it had been spent only in Naples and largely within the confines of Casa Materna. To 'Mamma' the thing that counted most was that she believed the whole of this fully-engaged life to have been lived under the direction of the Lord she loved.

At any hour of the day, until 1961, a tiny, white-haired man in a grey suit, his lined face creased as much with smiles as with care, would be found somewhere in the compound. Surrounded by little children, he was able to look down on them. When the older boys talked to him he looked up into their eyes. Riccardo Santi, shrinking with age towards the end of his life, never stood more than five feet and a few inches, yet he possessed none of the arrogance and self-assertiveness, the touchiness with which many small men compensate for their lack of stature. Indeed, his very equality of structure with the children emphasised much of his inner spirit. He was never childish, and yet, as disciples should be, he was always 'child-like'. His trust in God as His father, the firm simplicity of his religious beliefs and his lack of doubts, his gentleness, even his quiet voice, his tenacity and his joy in living all reflected this child-like side of his nature which, to the end, he never outgrew.

Religiously, the Italian term 'Evangelical' suited him more exactly than the more technical title, 'Protestant'. He was always more concerned to commend the Gospel of God's love in Christ than he was to argue about theological doctrines. Indeed, despite his theological training he remained inexpert in philosophical argument. He had a deep love for the Methodist Church; though he never really understood or appreciated the ways and beliefs of his Catholic neighbours, or cultivated the same friendships as did Teophilo and Fabio, he was less concerned to argue about the truth than to demonstrate it in his life and activity. To present him as anything less than an out-and-out Evangelical would be distortion; to allow this to imply the harshness and bitterness which often distinguish minority leaders would be equally false. Never, in his private conversation or his prayers, did he refer to his Catholic neighbours with anything but love.

There was one incident of his early ministerial career in Naples which illustrates these qualities admirably.

Albanella is a mountain village near Paestium and Evangelical work began there in the 1890s when an Italian emigrant to the U.S.A. returned home as a Protestant. Without any training he began to preach to his neighbours and gained ten or a dozen converts. The response was bitter persecution for the isolated community. The local priest, horrified at the defection from his church, called for Jesuit help in conducting a mission against heresy. In their turn a few of the villagers set out to seek a champion and came to Naples. In 1903 they found young Riccardo Santi and asked him to visit Albanella.

Riccardo responded at once. Any opportunity of declaring his faith was worth taking, and he rejoiced in the chance of preaching in the little *piazza* of the mountain village. There was much interest in the stranger, for the village saw few folk from the outside world, and Riccardo returned again and again. The

Evangelical community began to increase, and within a few years had grown to fifty. They decided to build their own church, and did so without guidance or architectural help. The result was a very curious building, the only Methodist church in Italy with a bell. Fearful and angry the priest approached the bishop in Salerno and a challenge was issued by the Jesuits to Pastor Santi to engage in a public debate. The subject chosen was 'Purgatory', a matter on which Riccardo had expressed decidedly Protestant, and therefore heretical, views. The *piazza* was crowded, and on a platform in the centre the robed Jesuits and the dark-suited Pastor argued through the day. Riccardo was no match for the professional theological arguments and could not counter the long references to traditional doctrine and the great Councils of the Church. It must be admitted, however, that many of the simple peasants could not follow the theological debate, either, and the Pastor's presentation of Gospel truth as he saw it won a good deal of acceptance. By the end of the day his courage and simplicity had gained many sympathisers and when he led the way to the odd little Methodist building there were many who followed him.

His victory appeared to be terribly vindicated. The leader of the Jesuit preaching-mission died of a coronary thrombosis during the night. The persecuted Protestants exulted. Their triumphant spirits were deflated, however, when Pastor Santi preached to them the same day, and in his words his true character was shown.

'This is not the work of God,' he insisted. 'Would this loving God of whom I spoke yesterday strike a man dead because he did not see the truth as I see it? God *never* works like this! If you believe that He does you have yet no clear vision of the God I preach, the God who healed the sick and raised the dead by Jesus Christ!'

For many years Riccardo continued to visit Albanella twice a month. It was an arduous and tiring journey, which had to be made by bus or train and involved leaving early one morning and returning the next night. But, if these simple people were to be taught the love of God, it was clear that they needed regular instruction. Unable to pay for a preacher of their own, he served them until 1926 when, because of the demands of Casa Materna on his time, Teofilo took over his father's duties of twice-monthly visitation and preaching. Teofilo, at this time, was just seventeen.

Riccardo Santi was, beyond all his other interests, a minister of the Methodist Church. He founded two churches in Naples and another in Portici, often returning to preach to his old congregations in the city. In the open air he was as much at home as he was in the pulpit. No one could have been better suited to conducting children's worship and he managed to deal with the most abstruse and difficult doctrines in a way they could understand. In preaching about the Trinity, for instance, he illustrated the perplexing dogma in this way.

'What was I yesterday morning when I was cutting your hair?'

'The barber,' came the answer from the whole chapel.

'And in the afternoon when I gave you castor oil?'

'The doctor'.

'And now, when I'm preaching here in the chapel?'

'Our *padrone* . . . the pastor.'

Riccardo beamed on them, their faces intent to know what would come next. 'But what am I all the time . . . even when I am preaching or cutting your hair? What do you call me?'

The response was loud and confident. 'Papa! Papa Santi!'

The preacher had made his point in a way they would remember. 'Always I am Papa, your father. But although I *am* Papa I am doctor, barber and preacher all in one, as well!'

Perhaps by their very nature, because of their individualism and their isolation, the Italian Evangelical churches tended to be separatist. From the beginning of his Naples ministry, however, Riccardo had felt himself charged to build up the ecumenical spirit before that word became a cliché of World Church jargon. He was one of the founders of the Society for Evangelical Unity amongst the Protestants of Naples. After the Second World War had ended the value of this particular work became clear. The Allied leaders found themselves at home in dealing with the Catholic Church, for in it they found much the same kind of organisation as existed in the armed services—a breakdown of responsibility with an overall authority. Protestants were less easy to confer with. There were too many groups and, very often, no one who could represent these diverse and often small communities. In Naples the matter was easier. The Protestant chaplains, feeling a responsibility for maintaining the witness of the Church, quickly discovered the existence of the Evangelical

Union and turned to Pastor Santi as its leading figure. One of the results was the holding of open-air services in Naples from the first Sunday after the 'liberation'.

Having said so much it still remains true that above all else Riccardo Santi was the friend of the children. From his first acceptance of Angelo and Rosetta not merely hundreds but thousands of children passed through his home. He never forgot the fact that when his widowed mother could no longer support him he was received and trained, both for his daily work and in the love of God, at the first Italian Protestant orphanage in Venice. His long life was spent in repaying that debt. 'As you yourself received help, so take these children', became the motto of his life.

Lasciate i fanciulli venire a me, the words incised in the stone façade of the old villa Monaco, must have sounded like Papa's very own personal invitation. 'Let the children come unto me.' And because he welcomed them with such compassionate love they came to the Lord he served.

Many times he said the same thing in the same words. 'When I see a child I do not ask who he is or where he came from. I become that child.'

That was the secret of his wonderful and dedicated life.

As he drew near its end he was happy to see Fabio dreaming finer dreams than he himself had ever dared to do. Not even his son's death left him hopeless, though it did leave him stricken, coming in the same year that he also lost his wife and his son-in-law in America. Teofilo was still there, and Emanuele, too. Together his sons would do more than he had ever done. Looking back he wrote this of his work.

As we turn to look at the road already trodden we see that it bears witness to the power of Christian faith in action. We feel that our mission has no conclusive endings, but only stages on a never-ending journey.

For his life-work he might have had many honours. After his help given to war-orphans in the first World War he refused an Order from the King of Albania because he could not believe that service ever merited public distinctions. He could have been honoured by the Italian King and the government, but he would not accept for the same reason. Then, in 1958, came an honour he could not well refuse, for it was given without his knowledge.

The American Overseas Association conferred its second award on him.

In the Assembly Hall of Casa Materna a distinguished company gathered together. The children were there in full complement. There were past students and local residents. Chaplains from the American forces were present, and high officials of the N.A.T.O. headquarters based in Naples, together with many other people who wanted to express their delight in this appreciation of his work.

The presentation was made by the United States Ambassador, who spoke in the highest terms of the life-work of the old man sitting quietly in the centre of the stage. Riccardo took the plaque in his hands. Like his voice as he replied, they trembled slightly. This was not a medal to pin on his coat. It was something which for many years would stand in Casa Materna itself. This was the inscription.

Honouring human kindness, benevolence and self sacrifice
International
Humanity Service Award
of the
American Overseas Association
Riccardo Santi
For years of faithful service
at Casa Materna Orphanage
which has been a home for so many
unfortunate and abandoned children
1958

The year 1961 dawned. Sixty years earlier he had arrived in Naples, and this year he would celebrate his ninetieth birthday. At Casa Materna it was never forgotten that Papa's birthday was also the birthday of Casa Materna itself. It was to share his birthday tea that the first children had gone home with him. Because of this it is always a festival day. This year it would be unforgettable. The entertainment, the hundreds of friends and old scholars, the music would hardly be able to express their joy.

But Papa never saw the anniversary.

In February he was very weak, though almost to the very end he had insisted on sharing one daily meal with the children.

EMANUELE COMES HOME

On Saturday, though he had been resting as much as Teofilo could persuade him to do, he came to a decision.

'Tomorrow I want to take the service of Holy Communion in the chapel. I don't want help. I would like to take it by myself.'

So to the Methodist congregation of Portici, Riccardo Santi offered the Sacrament for the last time. He led them through the familiar liturgy, his voice stronger than they recalled hearing it for many months. He distributed the elements and dismissed each group of communicants from the rail with a sentence of hope and confidence. Then, at last, he sat down to rest and Emanuele came forward to give the final blessing.

On Monday and Tuesday he was very tired, and stayed in bed. It was on Tuesday that he called his two sons to his bedside, taking their hands and looking at these men who, with Fabio, carried the burden of orphanage and school.

'I feel the time has come to hand over my responsibility. I can't do it any longer by myself.'

Teofilo looked at Emanuele and there was a hint of a smile in the eyes of them both.

One or other of them never left him. If Papa Santi had come to the moment when, even in his own mind, he was no longer responsible for his great family, it was clear he had come to the end of the task, but it was only on the Wednesday that Teofilo saw the first clear evidence of it. He went to the window and summoned Emanuele. By the time his brother reached the room Riccardo Santi's gracious spirit had slipped away. It was 1st February, 1961.

The news spread swiftly. This, indeed, was the passing of an age. The great leader of Protestantism in Italy was dead. There was no one else amongst them who could go back, as he could, linking the new days of Christian understanding with the very first year of religious liberty in modern Italy. But if some amongst the pastors and leaders of the Ecumenical Churches who sat in the Assembly Hall for his funeral service remembered these things, that was not their first thought. The service was a time of thanksgiving for a great life, nobly and selflessly lived. The crowds who thronged the streets to see the cortège pass to the little Protestant area of the Portici cemetery knew only one thought. Papa Santi was dead, and they would never quite see anyone like him again. These same crowds had mourned Fabio for many reasons. They wept as Papa's coffin passed them for one reason above all others. They had loved him.

It is the custom in Naples to pay tribute to the dead in a particular way. Friends or family will announce the death and the time and place of the funeral by posters, some twenty inches by twelve, which are pasted on walls, on hoardings or near the house concerned. These announcements include some statement of virtues and achievements by way of public testimony. No one strips them down afterwards. They remain until the sun bleaches them and the rain peels them away.

On the outer wall of Casa Materna, on the Corso Garibaldi, two fragments remain. One had been there for eight years when I saw it. It bore the name *FABIO* and the words which followed, all that remained of this public tribute, could be translated: *He poured out his life....*

Of the other even less was visible after three years. *RICCARDO SANTI* followed by the single word *Pastor*.

In each case, the little which remained was enough to characterise the man.

12

Casa Materna Today

However skillfully a writer may present his facts he can never adequately convey the atmosphere of Casa Materna. Colour can be imagined ... the old faded red of the villa; the green of the shutters and the shaded greens of lawns and bushes; the blue of smocks and dresses, darker than the brilliant blue of sky and bay. the sense of tranquility can be imagined, too ... old fountains with water gently running into leaden tubs of geraniums; a marble column here, an armless statue amongst the trees; the slow-moving farmer bending over the long rows of carnations; the quietness of the chapel, with the memory of Papa Santi's gentle voice. Noise, too, is there, muted by the summer heat ... the cry of hens by the red farm-house ... the dull burr of machines in the old stables ... the low, precise voices of Signora Livia and her daughter Daniela ... the chatter of children. Even the children themselves can come to life in our minds ... their concentration on some obscure game with coloured counters, invented by themselves, played on the roof of the wide verandah ... the sudden burst of staccato chatter ... the swift smile and outstretched hands in response to a question from Uncle Teofilo or Uncle Emanuele. These things can be imagined.

But some things can never be conjured up except in the memory of those who have stayed there—though even a day or two are sufficient to make such a memory indelible. Colour, scent, noise, even the way the children look—these are no more than the clothing of mood and atmosphere. Such words as peace, gaiety, purpose, faith are but attempts to capture intangible and immortal qualities—and yet each of these qualities is inherent in the life of Casa Materna. At this point the power of description fails. Casa Materna must not only be seen, but felt.

To see and feel it, if you ever go to Naples, you need only pass through the gateway of 235 Corso Garibaldi. You are in a different world from that which the tourist knows.

Just inside the gateway the porter's lodge is on the right and, opposite to it, a door leads into the chapel, once the stables of the Prince of Monaco. The wide marble staircase with a wrought-iron handrail leads to Dr Teofilo Santi's apartments on the first floor. The second floor is taken up with a series of apartments fairly recently converted into guestrooms. From time to time it houses conferences but, in the main, it is available to anyone interested in Casa Materna who may wish to stay there. On the ground floor of the building Dr Teofilo Santi has his consulting-rooms and surgery.

A few yards more, through the small patio, and you are in the grounds of Casa Materna itself. Unseen from this point, hidden behind the coach-house, now a garage, and the stables which have been turned into a machine-shop, is the red farmhouse surrounded by a cultivated field. Beside it are enclosures for hens, pigs and cows. It is the farmer's responsibility to tend another garden on the opposite side of the grounds which is full of flowers. Both fields are profitable. By an arrangement with the farmer, who is a Portici Methodist, the cost of all stock and seed is shared by himself and the Home. In the same way, half the proceeds of sale are shared. Much of the fresh vegetables used in the kitchens are produced here.

Neapolitans love flowers, and those grown here are of many kinds. Carnations in particular are readily saleable—and if the eighty long rows of carnations in this field were stretched in a single line they would reach for more than five miles! Little vases, gay with colour, are found throughout the home and especially, though it might seem surprising, in the boys' bedrooms.

The grounds cover seven acres, including the farm land, and the first buildings you come to after leaving the courtyard are those in which the older boys live and work. The carpentry building, a long block built as an extension to the Prince's tiny chapel, was opened in 1948. The radio and television workshop began in 1959, and the machine shop in 1960. The boy's residential block, with dormitories and large rooms for communal living and study, was the result of the Choir's tour of the United States in 1956, and was erected during 1957/8, a posthumous tribute to

Fabio's vision. Replanning of its accommodation will now bring more boys from the main block into it and relieve the congestion in the villa itself. The resident house-mother and house-father, who also works as a technical teacher, are Italian-speaking members of the Salvation Army.

The medical block, near the villa, was originally only one storey, built in 1946 after the return from Praiano, when medical care was a major necessity; the second storey was added by the generosity of a Swiss lady. Washed in the same red colour as the villa, it half faces the Bay, and the verandah and the steps leading up to the entrance are bathed with sunlight. There is accommodation for 25 or 30 patients, and rooms for two resident workers, who are usually young Americans giving voluntary service. There are few resident patients; perhaps a dozen or so who have to be isolated because of skin-troubles or some infection. There is a dentistry room and the local Medical Officer of Health visits the clinic each day.

On the opposite side of the compound from the medical block stands a solid-looking white building, shielded from the gardens by high bamboo screens. This is the school, with a large assembly hall, class-rooms and administrative offices. It was begun in 1952 and opened in 1954, almost 50 years after Ersilia Santi had begun her first kindergarten.

Despite education being compulsory for all Italian children, there is a considerable gap between what is on the statute-book and what is practically possible. Shortage of teachers and of accommodation, even in the cities, means that even where children go to school they can do so only in the morning or the afternoon. The same class-rooms and the same teachers have to cope with two different sets of children each day. In Naples, tens of thousands of children have no education at all and, by contrast, the opportunities offered at Casa Materna are enormous. There is full-day education in reasonably spacious class-rooms by teachers who have time to give themselves both to pupils and subjects. The 200 children resident in the Home are mostly below high school age or are more likely to profit from non-grammar-stream education, and are therefore to be found in their own school. In addition, 200 or more children come from the town of Portici itself, those who live at a distance being fetched and taken home in two bright blue buses with *Casa Materna* on their sides.

Junior children wear regulation blue smocks during school-hours, while the kindergarten children wear white. The school includes kindergarten classes and five elementary grades, and takes children up to junior high school standards. The class-rooms are clean, airy and tidy, and the classes themselves small by British standards. Voluntary help is often given by visitors, so that the whole building was recently cleaned and colour-washed by United States sailors and some of the class-rooms decorated with attractive murals by visiting French students. Text-books are those agreed by the Ministry of Education and tend to be all-inclusive, ranging through elementary history, geography, biology, mathematics and so on in the one book. They look bright, attractive and well-used, but any class turns away from its books as quickly as do children anywhere else in the world when a visitor enters the room, and bursts into uninhibited song at the first gesture of invitation from the teacher. Visual aids, being expensive, tend to be scarce.

Art and handwork are, of course, a normal part of the curriculum but the Casa Materna schools train the boys in a skill which is peculiarly Italian.

Torre del Greco is a sailor's town, but since the days of the Romans it has had a secondary industry—the making of cameos. They have been found in Herculaneum and Pompeii, as perfect as when these towns were overwhelmed, and from Roman times little boys in the small town have learned the skill from their fathers. Amongst the boys of Torre del Greco was Giovanni, who was brought to Riccardo Santi when his father died and his mother could no longer support him. Returning after Casa Materna had given him home and education he worked at the making of cameos, joined a local firm and eventually became its director, and it was through him that cameo-making became a subject on the art syllabus. Now, at a long bench against the sun-bright windows, a line of boys can be seen scraping at the hard shells, hopeful of creating the same exquisite designs as the great ladies of Herculaneum once wore.

The Roman craftsmen worked on hard gems, modern artists use the hard, spiky coverings of molluscs found in the Naples area and near the coasts of Sicily and Sardinia, and 'foreign' shells are imported from Madagascar and Japan. The shells are sawn open and then cut into small pieces from which part of the white outer crust is scraped away until the darker brown or reddish layer of the inner shell is exposed. It is in this arduous task that the true artist is seen. On the top shell is drawn the outline of the design and after the crust has been scraped away round this pattern it is then delicately chiselled to produce the exquisite relief of the cameo. Beginning by carving butterflies on lower quality shells the boys pass on to the classical Greek and Roman designs and heads. There is a growing market for genuine cameos amongst tourists and foreign importers and no one is more anxious to help the talented boys of Casa Materna than the wealthy man from Torre del Greco who was once a boy there himself.

All these other buildings are ancillary to the old villa.

The villa is larger than it was in 1920, with extensions to each side and a small room built above the second floor. Beyond the pillared verandah is a circular entrance porch, with marble busts and statues in the alcoves. Beyond it is an assembly room with a television set. To the right is a music room, again with a television set, the central offices in which Teofilo and Emanuele conduct the business of the Home and Emanuele's own flat. In the large office with wide windows and a sweeping view of the Bay stand Fabio's desk, carved bookcases and carved filing-cabinet. Here, too, are the more intimate Santi possessions linking present and past—the last pen-and-ink portrait of Papa Santi, drawn by Professor Elio Rinaldi of the University; photographs of the archway where Angelo and Rosetta sold their matches, of the first Naples houses and some of the first children, all fading a little with age; more pictures of Papa and Mamma, and of Fabio; the award of the American Overseas Association.

To the left of the main entrance are bathrooms and dormitories for the smaller boys. On the first floor are the girls' dormitories and their study-rooms where homework is done. Here, too, is 'the Nest'—sleeping rooms, playroom and bathrooms for the kindergarten dedicated in 1959 to the memory of Mamma Santi. Outside the girls' rooms is the wide balcony above the pillared entrance, where with books, toys or dolls some of the girls are always to be found outside of school hours.

The small storey above contains workrooms and sewing-rooms

for the girls. In the basement, which opens on to a wide concrete playground set out for ball games, are the kitchens and dining rooms.

To the office which Papa used to call the 'harbour', knowing that all his children would arrive there some time, comes a constant stream of callers and a mound of daily mail. Much of the mail and many of the callers have the same intention—to persuade the already crowded home to make room for 'just one more child'. It is impossible to accede to more than a small proportion of the requests, for of these 2,000 applications a year only 40 or 50 can normally be accepted. Religion is never a factor in the decision. One question alone is of paramount importance. 'How great is this child's need?'

Sometimes there is no need at all, only a wish that a child should have the privilege of being there. So it was with two elderly people who entered the office with two small children. They greeted Emanuele with grave pleasure.

'These are our grandchildren.'

'They are a credit to you.'

'It is kind of you to say so, for in that case they are a credit to Casa Materna. You know that we were children here ourselves many years ago? We married after we left the Home and then because we had not enough money to care for our children Papa Santi took them, too.'

Emanuele nodded and the old man went on. 'That is why we want our grandchildren to come here.'

'But surely their parents are not poor, as you were?'

The old people looked affronted. 'Certainly not. They will pay for them. But we, and they, want the children to begin life with the same advantages that *we* had!'

It took some time to persuade them that it was the parents' duty to care for the children at home. Even then they would not be consoled until it was agreed that at least they might attend the school.

The need of others is only too apparent.

'Frog' was a little boy of six, whose father had finally died as a result of war wounds. What does a woman with five children and no money do in such circumstances? State aid was non-existent. Friends have children of their own. 'Frog's' mother brought the ungainly little boy with his big head and awkward gait to Casa Materna, and two other children with him, both younger than himself.

Paola's father died of tuberculosis. In the overcrowded single room it was not surprising that her sister contracted the same disease. To provide medical help for the child the mother had to work, and then spend almost all her earnings on medicine. Paola, too, found her way to Casa Materna.

So did Maria, whose father and mother were separated. There were six children. The father took five of them and left his wife to care for Maria. Then the mother fell ill and was unable to care for even one child. Neighbours brought her to the Santis—and how can you hand back such a child to the neighbours?

In one recent month there were seven admissions, including three little brothers. The father had gone to one of the big towns to look for work. The mother, finding the burden too great, deserted the family who were taken in by their grandparents. Then the grandmother died. What would an old man do with three little boys unless there were some such home as this willing to take them in?

That same month Filippo arrived from Palermo. He was thin, dirty, bruised and frightened. Taught by a drunken father to beg and steal, when his 'earnings' were insufficient to buy drink the besotted man flung him out into the street and chased him away. Filippo was seven years old.

Time after time the same sort of tragic tale is told, sometimes by a minister whose pastoral work has led him to neglected children in city slums or some mountain village, often by angry neighbours or a distraught mother or father. In the office, where a little girl was not long ago accepted because she staged a sit-down strike on the floor until she knew she could stay, the stories are unravelled, the lies sorted out from the truth, the distortions-for-effect discounted, the harsh actuality of the situation uncovered. Almost every child is in need of food, medicine, hope, values. Most of all these sad-faced, frightened little children are in need of love. That, above all else, is what they find as they settle into the big family.

How sad it is that so many must be turned away.

Admission ages range from 3 to 8 years, and many children

remain until they have finished their technical or grammar-school education at the age of 16 or 17. But not all, unfortunately.

A sharp-faced man appeared in the office one morning, demanding in a North Italian accent to see his two neices, who had been at Casa Materna since their father and mother had died. Now they were about 13 and 14.

'What do you want with them?'

'I want to take them home. To Milan.'

'Why?'

'My wife is not well. I have to go out to work. They must come and look after their aunt and the house.'

'But what about their education? They are doing well at school. They should stay for two or three years longer to make the most of it.'

The man laughed. 'Why educate girls? They know enough to sweep floors and cook meals, don't they?' He stood up, his face angry. 'Bring them at once. You can't stop me taking them! I am their next of kin.'

It was only too true, and not a few other girls are removed in the same way. Unknown relatives, sometimes a father who has spent years in prison or a mother who has passed beyond the service of the streets, may appear and snatch children back from a happy home into a life of servitude. Casa Materna has served its purpose.

Fortunately it happens less often than it might and even when it does the child will go out knowing how to use time as well as skill, having seen visions and shared a purposefulness which only true Christian home-life can give.

The day begins for the children at 6.30 a.m. or half an hour later in the cold months of January and February. In the hour and a half before breakfast at 8.0 they tidy their rooms, clean the floors and do the simple chores of the house. Self-help is the rule. But even before breakfast life is neither silent nor dull. From boys' and girls' dormitories and from the music room come the sounds of flutes, trumpets, drums, piano and horns. Breakfast consists of coffee or milk with bread. If this sounds austere it should be added that the bread is excellent, and many poor children have no more than this for a whole day.

At 8.45 there is a brief act of worship. Classes begin at 9.0.

At 10.0 the blue buses, escorted by older boys, arrive with the non-resident children and they come leaping out eagerly in their blue or white smocks. Lunch is at 1.0 o'clock—a free meal for the non-residents—and for the Casa Materna residents there is the added luxury of a second meal at night. Soup, followed by pasta or meat or fish, and then by fruit, would be a sumptuous meal in many homes from which these children come. There is good water to drink and plenty of bread for those who are still hungry.

At 2.0 or a little later the kindergarten go to rest, the first five grades return to school and the older boys go off to the workshops where, if they wish, they may continue to work long after the other children have left. At 6.30 there is dinner—a menu much like lunch—and from 8.0 onwards homework has to be done before bedtime.

Emanuele can recall being put to sit at a bench by himself in his local school because he refused to repeat the *Ave Maria*. There is no discrimination, no religious compulsion of this kind in the school. He can also remember weeks and months when the diet provided by Papa and Mamma was no more than spaghetti and weak soup, and he would walk along the Via Duomo in Naples looking through windows where men sat at supper, and wonder what it felt like to have enough to eat. For those who belong to the family now it is a changed world indeed.

The word 'family' is inevitable, and 'Home' has no overtone of institutionalism.

Older children are made responsible for smaller ones. In the dormitories, where there are often between sixteen and twenty beds, they are arranged on the 'bunk' principle, and the older child, sleeping above, has to act as 'big brother' or 'sister' to the smaller one below. This 'family' feeling comes naturally because *everyone* is part of the family. Voluntary workers from overseas are quickly drawn into it. A stranger, staying for a day or so, gets a hug and a goodnight kiss with the same naturalness as do the Santis themselves. But it is they, the Santi family, around whom everything revolves. It would not occur to them to eat any meal but breakfast in their own apartments. For the rest, they sit at table, often surrounded by guests, in the big dining-room. 'Uncle' Teofilo and 'Uncle' Emanuele are not the 'principals' of an establishment. They have been part of Casa Materna from the day they were born and can never grow out of it. Signora Livia is no mere teacher or housekeeper; she is becoming more and more what Mamma herself was, the mother of them all. Daniela sits with the girls, and one of them, an orphan, lives with her in the Santi apartments.

Discipline is no more difficult than in any other home. There is little need of punishment where there is love.

Feeding the family is a considerable operation and, with a doctor as Director, special thought is given to providing a balanced as well as an appetising diet. There are six cooks at work in the kitchen, over which Signora Livia exercises constant supervision. The total food consumed by 200 children in the Home and more than that number of non-residents is immense. 200 pounds of bread a day, 100 pounds of macaroni, in some form or other, 100 pounds of meat each week and the same amount of fresh fish. Vegetables come from the farm when they are in season: for the rest of the time they must be bought in the market. Not even at Casa Materna is fruit grown. 'Even *this* family would harvest its own,' said Emanuele, with a smile.

Daily bargaining and stocking-up in the market is eased because an ex-Casa Materna boy is one of the market officials and arranges that what is needed is stacked ready when the wagon arrives.

In the dining-room, down in the big basements, religion is seen to be a natural part of family life. Over the three arches are painted these words.

Cristo e' il capo do questo casa.
Christ is the head of this house.
Cristo e' l'ospite invisibile di ciaocun pasto.
Christ is the unseen guest at every meal.
Cristo e' l'uditore silenzioso di ogni conversazione.
Christ is the silent listener to every conversation.

Grace is always said before meals, and always by a child.

At the end of supper come family prayers, taken again by the children. Teofilo or Emanuele calls for silence from the archway near their table, and then holds a child before him. He reads from the Italian version of the famous devotional booklet *The Upper Room*, while the child stands silent. The reading gives an opportunity for encouragement or admonition, sometimes for a gentle rebuke. After the reading news is shared—guests introduced, part of a letter read from a boy or girl who has left. Then eyes are closed and hands folded. The boy or girl repeats a prayer he or she has written and learned. The language is simple, the voice sharp and taut, the petitions natural and the whole tenor of the prayer intimate and personal. Even the kindergarten children share in the devotions, for sometimes four or five little boys will stand together and repeat the Lord's Prayer in high-pitched, eager voices.

When the meal is over and plates are cleared away the smallest children leave the room first. But before they do so they come quietly to the Santi family table, passing from one to another with a hug and a goodnight kiss.

'*Buon*' *notte!*' The little voices are already sleepy as some give the familiar farewell.

Most content themselves with the more common phrase, '*Ciao!*'

The tiny white-smocked infants slip out of the door. Before the 'uncles' or guests, who have waited to see the other girls and boys leave, can climb the stairs to 'the Nest', the little ones are tucked up in bed and fast asleep.

Because religion is part of life to these children Sunday is never a dull day. It begins quietly, with a later breakfast than usual. At 10.0 there is Sunday School and this is followed by a simple children's service in the chapel, where Teofilo plays the organ. Then, until the evening service at 5.0 they are quite free. The girls change into their best dresses, the boys into their blue woollens, the kindergarten into bright red ones. After lunch there are games and, being Italy, footballs appear in the concrete playground by the dining room and outside the bigger boys' building. A straggle of visitors makes its way through the gateway into the ground, loaded with parcels of sweetmeats, food and fruit. For once in the week, some of the children do not seem hungry at suppertime!

For the children, Sunday-after-supper brings freedom from work and an hour or so with television. For the Santi family, as often as possible, the still rarer treat of a ride into Naples, an ice-cream at Motta's or a quiet walk by the sea.

Like any other school, there are vacations at Christmas, when many children go to parents, relatives or friends for a five-day break, and at Easter, for two weeks. In the summer, when heat makes schoolwork almost impossible, the vacation lasts from the beginning of June to 1st October. Only a few of the children go home. Mornings are spent on the black-sanded beach, reached from the villa by a tunnel under the railway. In the afternoon there are athletics, games or quiet activities like sewing, while older boys often choose the workshops. There are excursions, too—to Pompeii, Herculaneum and the many museums of Naples.

It is during this period that Casa Materna is open to less fortunate children. Slum children are welcomed to the beach and to a midday meal. Children from the political refugee camps may have a fortnight away from the barbed wire which surrounds them for the rest of the year. Children from Protestant villages—such as San Sebastian, in L'Aquila, a village untouched by the sun in its cleft-like valley—have a 'break' in the sunshine by the sea.

In other ways, too, Casa Materna shares its own happiness. There is a huge Christmas party, with an entertainment twice repeated for all who wish to come. Then, on the Sunday nearest to June 12th, Papa Santi's birthday and the foundation day of Casa Materna, comes the Anniversary. A tremendous affair, there are entertainments by the children, music by the band, songs by the choir, stalls of goods for sale, and—perhaps most welcome of all—the reunion of hundreds of past students and members of the Home. Helpers and well-wishers of all sorts come, too, from Portici and Naples, and especially from the Americans associated with N.A.T.O. headquarters. Their presence emphasises the strong association of Casa Materna and the United States. This link is historic and has been effectively strengthened by all that has happened since the war. It is a pity that, even now, so few people in Britain know the Casa Materna story or respond to its needs in the same way as the Americans.

From the very beginning, when Papa Santi came to Naples, American help has been continuous. From the day Fabio approached an American chaplain, immediately after the 'liberation', seeking help for the children in Praiano, it has increased. Children were invited to visit the American camps and warships. An American Red Cross worker returns each year to Portici to give some secretarial help, because the Casa Materna children, in 1945, 'made a Merry Christmas for 20,000 American G.I.s who wanted to be home'. Other examples of this association between the Home and men who have served in Naples, chaplains and officers at N.A.T.O. headquarters, sailors who are based on the port, friends who knew Emanuele in the States or heard the choir sing on its tour in 1956, multiply year by year. 'News Briefs' in the *Casa Materna News* draw attention to some of them.

'A truckload of medical supplies, including cod liver oil, cough syrup, castor oil and other items... was donated by the P.X. through the American chaplains.'

'Recently a circulating library was made possible through contributions of the Protestant Women of the Chapel connected with N.A.T.O. in Naples. The table, like the shelves, was made in our carpentry workshops.'

There are many other notes of the same kind, but gifts from those stationed in Naples are a response to love as well as need, because it is impossible for a lonely man to go into Casa Materna without feeling enriched, or a family to go for a meal without finding their family circle immeasurably increased.

Fabio Santi once wrote: 'The greatest gift Casa Materna can give to a child is love. The spirit of love is one of the two great cornerstones on which Casa Materna is built. The other is the spirit of faith, based on the love of Jesus Christ.'

Love, service, happiness and religion can no more be separated in Casa Materna than the constituent elements of the air the children breathe. The chapel and evening prayers in the dining-rooms are the very centre of its life. Yet there is no 'compulsory religion' here, and the expressions of faith may be quiet or gay. Reminiscent of the '*jongleur* of Notre Dame', a small boy asked before a concert given in the chapel—'Can I play my drums in there to the glory of God?' He had no doubt of the answer.

Here at Casa Materna the old dictum is completely true. 'Religion is caught, not taught.'

Three questions remain. What happens to the children when they leave? How is Casa Materna governed? What are its needs?

Casa Materna always has more boys than girls, but both groups tend to find work in ordinary commercial and industrial life, while a few become gardeners. Since the machine-shop has been opened, an increasing number have become industrial apprentices, and the radio and television workshops offer boys a trade which fits into an expanding industry. Big engineering and electrical firms such as Olivetti or the electronics industries are glad to consider boys of integrity who have already had some technical training. A knowledge of English is a great help, and boys from the technical workshops as well as those doing academic courses are eager to learn—and to practise it with visitors.

Some are more adventurous. If quota restrictions did not prevent their emigration to the United States, that is undoubtedly the country many of them would choose. As it is, they move to other parts of Italy or even to Switzerland. Near Berne, for instance, is a little colony of more than twenty Casa Materna students working in engineering shops.

Not a few make their way in commerce and business. Others turn to the professions. Many become school-teachers. Not long ago two young men took their qualifying examinations in medicine in the same year at one of the Naples hospitals. Others had preceded them and more will follow. Four have become ministers of the Methodist church, and still others have chosen professions as diverse as architecture and seamanship.

For girls the choice has always been restricted. Certificates are needed if a girl is to become a seamstress or a dressmaker, and for many years girls have been trained for these trades. Others go into shops and offices. Opportunities in the professions in Italy still lag behind much of Western Europe and America and girls too seldom have the advantage of the further education given to boys. But a Casa Materna girl who has become a social caseworker is an example of possible new careers. The School now has commercial and secretarial courses and one girl, who had won a year's scholarship to the U.S.A., was chosen for high-grade confidential secretarial work in N.A.T.O. out of 300 applicants.

The important thing, however, is not what work is chosen by those who leave, but the fact that they bring to medicine, commerce, engineering or the making of their own homes that sense of integrity which every country so greatly needs today. Casa Materna teaches many subjects, but one of its greatest claims may properly be that it gives to those who live and study there deeply-rooted Christian values.

The government of Casa Materna has inevitably become more complex than in the days of Riccardo and Ersilia Santi. There is an annual General Assembly of the committees in each of the main supporting countries—the U.S.A., Switzerland and Britain. Drs Teofilo and Emanuele Santi, as Directors, have freedom of action but are responsible to two bodies—the General Assembly of Casa Materna and the Conference of the Methodist Church in Italy, to which it presents an annual report. Few governing bodies could be more understanding and helpful. Equally, few organisations have sounder or better qualified Directors to whom affairs can safely and discreetly be left.

The needs of Casa Materna can be set out fairly simply in terms of money, though the cost of living continually increases. With some 200 resident children and more than that number of non-residents there is a total staff of approximately 50. This includes teachers, cooks, farm workers and so on. In fact, much of the staff, like the temporary nurses and secretarial assistants from the U.S.A., is on an almost voluntary basis, and it also includes young men in training about the grounds and buildings. For the whole establishment the budget is approximately 125,000 dollars (say, £40,000) a year.

None of the children who are resident pay anything at all, and so have to be completely supported. A few, but not many, of the school-children pay comparatively small fees.

Rates, taxes, repairs, a small publicity account for the *Casa Materna News*, equipment for the workshops and living accommodation, meals for those who spend holidays at Portici from the slums, maintenance of the buses, postage to correspondents who never include stamped addressed envelopes, and a host of other items continue to push up the expenditure account.

There is no assistance from the State and all support has to come from the national supporting Societies or from individuals.

The principal need of Casa Materna therefore continues to be *money*. Two others are *clothing* and *food*. *All* kinds of clothing—but especially for boys rather than girls. Girls dresses are more easily made than boys' trousers, and the need for trousers, jeans, boys' sweaters and shirts continues unmet. Remember that most of the boys are small. *Food* is more difficult to define, but includes tinned food of every kind, cheese, condensed milk, jams and preserves.

One most useful way of helping and, at the same time, maintaining a personal link is by *sponsoring*. A sponsor may undertake financial responsibility for one child for about 200 dollars (£70) a year (though the figure is liable to fluctuate). This promotes a personal contact with a child; the opportunity of writing and (sometimes) having letters back. It can occasionally be usefully followed up by taking the child into the sponsor's own home abroad for a year.

Voluntary workers? This is the most attractive way of helping, for the worker comes to know Casa Materna better than in any other way—but it also has the largest number of difficulties. The volunteer will have to live away from home and not worry about it. There will be no luxuries, and not a great deal of free time. Time, like love, belongs to the children. Such a volunteer should be prepared to give two years to the work and, because it is an inhibiting business to spend the first six months gaining a rudimentary knowledge of Italian, it is becoming essential that there should be some slight acquaintance with the language before arrival.

The main categories of voluntary help are nurses, social workers, nursery workers, and men or women with technical skills which they can teach to older children. They will not make much out of the experience financially; only full board and limited pocket money. In other ways, they may gain more vision, faith and love than in any other ten years of their lives!

Those who wish for further information may write direct to *Casa Materna, 235 Corso Garibaldi, Portici, Naples, Italy.*

Or to the national Societies in Britain or America. In Britain Casa Materna is represented by the *Bible Lands Society, 33 Museum Street, London, W.C.1*. In America, by the *Casa Materna Society, Inc., Post Office Box 176, Tuckahoe, New York.* Contributions may be forwarded to either of the above addresses.

But the Santi Story does not end with an account of the work at Casa Materna, as the last three chapters of this book will show.

13

The Camp and the Caves

FOR the end of the Santi story—though 'end' is an inaccurate word for something which continues to grow and to initiate new ventures—we have to pick up the threads of Teofilo Santi's life from chapters 8 and 9. At that time he was Port Military Doctor in Naples, living alone, or with Fabio, at Casa Materna. He was able to remain in Naples throughout the war because he had an excellent working knowledge of German and English. With Naples ever more full of German soldiers, and a regular flow of British prisoners-of-war through the port, the presence of an officer fluent in both languages was invaluable. To many of the prisoners his helpfulness came as a surprise. He was not merely a hospital doctor and an Italian officer; he was also a Christian, deeply distressed about the war because he had friends in opposing camps, who found it difficult to distinguish between ally and enemy when he saw a man in need.

There was, for instance, the young prisoner who was undergoing the normal procedure of 'de-lousing' and disinfection on arrival at the port, while his stained uniform was treated in the fumigation chamber. From the opposite end of the building, Teofilo heard the sound of argument and went to investigate. The Italian guard was shouting furiously and trying to grab something which the boy was holding behind his naked back.

'*Tutti! Tutti!*' yelled the guard. 'Everything!'

The boy shouted back in English and the guard made a lunge at the prisoner's arm as Teofilo appeared.

'*Silenzio!*' he snapped at the guard. 'Now', he turned to the soldier, 'what have you got there? Everything has to be fumigated. The guard is quite correct.'

The boy stared at him, and then spoke diffidently. One did not argue with enemy officers. 'It's my Bible, sir,' he explained. 'It's been everywhere with me. If it goes into the fumigation tank it will just come to pieces. I ... I don't want to lose it, major.'

Teofilo turned to the guard. 'Fumigate everything else, but leave this out. It can't carry much infection. Give it to him when he has his uniform back.' He looked again at the astonished prisoner. 'Keep it with you, boy. Keep on reading it every day. Remember that your enemies read it, too. The truth as it is in Jesus is our only hope.'

Soon new prison-camps were built for the thousands of men captured in the Italian advance towards Alexandria and Suez, and any officer who could speak English was doubly useful. It was not long before Teofilo found himself with an additional appointment at the prisoner-of-war camp at Capua.

Capua is an old town, some thirty-five miles from the coast, on the road to Rome. The shops in the *piazza* are shaded by arcades. The domed churches dominate the houses clustering round them. The *piazza del Duomo*, quiet in peace-time, now echoed to the nailed boots and loud voices of soldiers in uniform as they stumped off to the bars and cafés. Just beyond the old town ran the Volturno river, where Garibaldi had finally defeated the King of Naples, now crossed by a broad bridge.

Less than a mile away, separated from the town by flat brown fields, was the prisoner-of-war camp. Surrounded by high barbed-wire fences broken only by a few heavily-guarded gates and a succession of towers with machine-guns mounted on them, the camp lived its own life. While men and women in Capua went freely about their business the prisoners existed in nissen huts, answered the daily roll-calls, swore resentfully because they were out of the war, or made the most of their forced leisure with a curriculum of talks, lectures and discussions. The impersonal blare of the brassy loud-speakers provided a constant interruption to all they did. In the camp church, a hut with a cross on the roof above the door, the chaplains conducted daily prayers and worship on Sundays. Each night, while towns and villages were blacked-out, Capua camp was brilliantly illuminated to prevent its being accidently bombed by invading aircraft.

Here in Capua Major Teofilo Santi had uninterrupted access to the camp, where he acted as one of the medical advisers. His knowledge of English relieved the difficulties of officers dealing ineffectively with guards who spoke only Italian. With the chaplains in particular he found a fellowship that transcended the enmities of war, and though, to himself and the prisoners, he remained an Italian soldier doing his military duties, his Christian faith and compassion illuminated all he did.

He had no idea, when he was first posted there, how long his association with the camp at Capua would last.

News from the North African front filtered into the camp with each fresh batch of prisoners. To soldiers who had seen Wavell holding grimly to an ever-decreasing area of Egyptian desert, the stories of Montgomery's bloody repulse of the Italians and Germans at el Alamein was heartening indeed. The subsequent drive towards Tripoli and the wiping out of Rommel's panzer forces gave the prisoners something new to wager on—the date and place of the Eighth Army's invasion of the Italian mainland. The news of the Sicilian and Salerno landings had a clear influence on their treatment by the Italian guards, and made them more certain that Italy would soon be out of the war. The only question was: 'When?'

Then, on 8th September, 1943, came the news they had all been waiting for. After just over three years of war the Italian Government had capitulated. An armistice was agreed. In the camp the prisoners went wild with delight. Amongst the Italian soldiers quartered in the town relief was mixed with anxiety. Their own government had surrendered. But what about the Germans? It was certain that they would intensify their defence of the country, yielding it to the invaders only mile by mile. While they harried every tiny advance of the British and Americans from Salerno to Naples, they were already retreating to new positions inland. Monte Cassino was heavily fortified with Nazi artillery. When it became impossible to hold on to Naples any longer they must retreat up the road that led through Capua to Rome.

In their headquarters the invading forces were already making plans to contain the Germans south of the river Volturno. A clear instruction was issued.

'The Volturno bridge at Capua *must* be destroyed.'

On the night of the armistice Teofilo was sitting with three fellow army-doctors in one of the houses they used as a medical mess, not far from the piazza del Duomo. 'Well,' commented one of them, 'I suppose the Camp is finished, and the prisoners will be off to fight somewhere else. Poor devils!'

'They seem happy enough at the thought of it.' Even now the noise there had not been completely silenced.

'What about us? Out of uniform, and back to our proper job?'

'If the job's still there. Major Santi's lucky.' The commanding officer looked at Teofilo. 'You'll go back to Casa Materna, I suppose?'

Teofilo nodded. His heart was lighter than it had been for years, but already a physical reaction was setting in. He looked terribly tired, as they all did. The war seemed to have stripped him of flesh and his dark, bright eyes were deeply sunk in his dark face. 'Yes. But I'll tell you what I'm going to do now, colonel; I'm going back to my room in the house next door and I'm going to bed. What's more, for the first time since the war began, I'm going to sleep late in the morning!'

All four doctors laughed as Teofilo went to the door. It was a good idea; the best way of celebrating that tired men could think of. In the camp, too, the prisoners went to sleep at last. The cafés and bars in Capua emptied. Men stumbled home, shaking their heads in bewilderment. It was a strange feeling, to be at peace.

German forces continued their rearguard action in the hills between Salerno and Naples.

Round the prison camp the arc lights burned brilliantly, marking out the rectangle that must never be bombed.

On the airfields the great bombers took their destructive loads aboard while pilots and navigators received their final briefing.

Then, in the darkest hours of the night, the bombers rose and swung inland. It seemed only a matter of minutes before they saw the arc-lights blazing in the plane below. Near by, the town of Capua huddled by the gleaming line of the Volturno river. Wave after wave of bombers dipped towards the little town, dropped their loads and roared up again into the night sky. The ground, trembling with the vibration of the planes above, leapt and split as the bombs fell. Impersonal, unvindictive, the aircraft dived, passed and returned, until the last bomb was dropped.

'Mission accomplished.'

The bombers' report was succint and accurate. The line of

escape had been smashed. The Volturno bridge was destroyed. So, too, was Capua.

Teofilo wakened at the first tremor of the approaching aircraft but he had no time to get out of the house before the bombs began to drop. He heard the crash of falling houses, the crunch of the bombs, the roar of the explosions and the spattering of wreckage as it fell in the streets and the piazza. Then, almost at once, the house was hit. Roof, floors and walls hurtled down on him and he waited for death.

At dawn, miraculously, he was still alive. His uniform was torn and filthy and he had a cut on his finger. That was all. Slowly, in case he was killed by new falls of masonry, he crawled out of the wrecked house. The sun hurt his eyes, and he rubbed the dust out of them as he looked where the house next door had stood. It was smashed to rubble. No one could have been in it and still live. Only one sound came from all over the town; the sound of crying. Cries of fear and agony; cries for help; cries for the dead.

He stood benumbed, tears rolling down his cheeks. He was alive, and he was a doctor. But what could one doctor do? In Capua seven thousand people were dead.

Those terrible still moments after he first crawled into the ruins of the devastated town were decisive in Teofilo's life. He was just thirty-four years old. He might easily have been crushed or blown to death like the thousands who had perished in the night, and yet he was alive. Why? As he set out to round up a few soldiers and do what he could to succour the living the question hammered at him. Why should *he* live? As he raced off to the camp hospital to get what medical supplies he could, it still rang in his mind. Chance? The Providence of God? Providence, when so many good, simple, faithful people had died? There was no clear answer. Instead, there came a growing conviction.

'I felt as if I had been born again . . . as if I had been given a new life . . . a life to use for others.'

Henceforth there could be no personal pride in his achievements; no resting; no relaxing; only a relentless driving forward of such purposes as God might reveal as his proper task. This service of thanksgiving was to be offered in the deep caves of Naples, in the slums and in the creating of a new kind of hospital. But first it was to be given in the camp.

As the war receded towards Rome a strange kind of peace descended on southern Italy, a peace terrible in its fatalistic acceptance of devastation. Farms, vineyards, homes, villages, towns had been destroyed in the battles that raged from Sicily northwards, and in the snow-bound stalemate of the long winter that followed. The buildings at Portici were occupied by the invading Army. Naples was in ruins. Discharged from his army service, Teofilo found himself fully occupied at Capua prison camp, put to use for German prisoners immediately the British and Commonwealth prisoners were released. Here his fluency in German made him as useful as he had been amongst the British, and he continued to serve there until the Germans, too, were dispersed and the camp stood empty.

It was not empty for long.

In the final stages of the war, as British, Americans and Russians drew nearer to the heart of Germany, a new problem had become evident. In the liberated countries of Central and Eastern Europe the 'resistance movements' came into the open and unhesitatingly declared their Communist allegiance. Populations which had managed to survive under the Nazis began to realise that they would have to spend the rest of their lives under Marxist rule. To some, the Communist ideology was as terrible as that of the Nazis had been, and they determined to escape. A few began to make their slow, pitiful way into Austria and Italy, until the first trickle of political refugees became a stream of families escaping, often in great peril, through the forests and over the mountains from Yugoslavia, Hungary and Rumania.

It was impossible for the Italian Government or the Allied Military Command to allow political refugees to roam at will over the country. Food was already appallingly scarce. Unemployment, always a problem in Italy, was becoming acute. The Communists, emerging as a powerful pressure-group in the big towns and the industrial north, had no compassion for those who fled from Communism in other countries. The refugees were herded into the old prison-camps, and new ones were built to accommodate them. The Italian Government wished to see them settled as soon as possible in any land that would take them. The military authorities were anxious to 'screen' them, to discover their real political affiliations and to find out all they could about countries now likely to be hidden by an 'iron curtain'. Only a few people, it seemed, were concerned about the personal welfare of these homeless and stateless people. Amongst the compassionate few was an organisation that had come into existence just after the end of the war—the World Council of Churches.

It was as a welfare officer of the W.C.C. in Geneva that Teofilo Santi found the gate of the camp opening to him once more. Now, however, there were not only the refugees at Capua who needed his help. Four more camps were opened—at Sant' Antonio, Pogano, Averso and Mercatello. In each there were about 500 or 600 people and his task was to look after the interests of all non-Catholics. Since this included Orthodox and Muslims, both of whom came in considerable numbers from Yugoslavia, Rumania, Albania and Hungary, the task was a heavy one indeed.

There were many problems, almost all of them emerging starkly as soon as the possibility of resettlement and emigration became a reality. Families were separated. Husbands had trekked out of their homelands without wives or children. Wives had lost touch with husbands, and sometimes it was almost impossible to discover whether they were alive or dead. Occasionally the cause was plainly desertion. Muslims might well have more than one wife, creating a situation unacceptable to countries prepared to receive refugee families. The deplorable state of health of many of the refugees was a constant concern to a welfare officer who was also a doctor; and the needs of children whose parents died or deserted them naturally weighed heavily on one whose whole early life had been spent in a family of children in similar case.

A limited number were settled in Italy itself. Others were resettled in Australia, New Zealand, America or the Scandinavian countries. A few of the children found their way, from time to time, to Casa Materna. The problems accumulated, seemingly insoluble. Some proved so, to the end; most were eased by understanding, firmness and compassion. Rigid rules were slowly bent as Teofilo and his colleagues went on hammering at one authority after another. Characters which had disintegrated through years of war, with the duplicity, meanness and sometimes crime which it bred, were slowly rebuilt. Many achieved a new integrity; some found a fresh reality of religious faith.

Teofilo, involved every day in the costly business of caring for those who had almost lost hope, was not alone. There were other workers appointed by the World Council of Churches, and his deputy was another ex-Army officer, Colonel Paolo Nitti. It is a family name which has already appeared in the Santi story. The colonel's father was the Methodist pastor who had taken over the Via Cimbri church from Riccardo Santi. It was Paulo Nitti's brother Giuseppe who had been imprisoned on Lipari as a left-wing rebel and it was because of Giuseppe's letter from Paris that Papa had first been arrested. Teofilo Santi and Paulo Nitti were as firm friends as their fathers had been, and their close association has continued through the later Santi projects. A short, impulsive-seeming man with a pointed black beard and shrewd eyes, Colonel Paulo Nitti carried on in the slowly-decreasing camps when Teofilo returned to Casa Materna and his private practice in Naples.

In time most of the camps were closed as the refugees were resettled through the unremitting labour of the W.C.C.'s Refugee Service workers all over the world. Capua camp still remains open and Colonel Nitti continues his work there, though most of those who now wander about the dusty pathways or huddle into the little rooms in the nissen huts are Muslim or Orthodox Yugoslavs, and many are 'hard core' cases for whom there seems little hope. Now and again when Teofilo visits it to renew acquaintances amongst its people or to discuss his new hospital with Paolo Nitti he looks across the fields to the little town, its houses, churches, bridge and piazzas rebuilt . . . to Capua, where he was born again.

One of the first official visitors to Naples was Dr Elmer Severinghaus who arrived soon after the armistice to study health conditions in the city. He was sent by the U.S. Government as a result of the report by senior officers on German and American devastation and destruction. Dr Severinghaus, who later became a director of the Medical Research Centre in New York, was a Congregationalist. He helped, a little later, to found 'Congregational Christian Service' to assist in reconstruction work in post-war Europe—an organisation which was soon to play an important part in one of Teofilo Santi's new ventures. In Britain, though it gave all possible help, essentials were severely rationed and material damage was desperately heavy. Germany, France and the Netherlands found their economies in parlous condition. The

Communist countries of Eastern Europe were increasingly alienated from the West. It was from across the Atlantic that money, material goods, food and medical aid came in large quantity. Italian links with America had always been peculiarly strong, and Dr Severinghaus set himself to do what he could to assist the Neapolitan people. His report not only confirmed those which had already been made. It showed them to have been a very tentative estimate of the destruction and physical deterioration which was to be seen throughout the city.

As a result of his representations a team of seven doctors was sent out from the United States to begin rehabilitation projects. One of them, Dr Kellerman, had a special instruction from Dr Severinghaus himself.

'Make sure to meet Dr Teofilo Santi.'

It was not only the Americans who were concerned about the Neapolitan people. A small Ecumenical Medical Committee had been set up soon after Teofilo returned from Capua, of which he himself was the leading member. It was essential to offer medical assistance as near to the centre of the city as possible, and to offer it freely. Premises in the half-ruined city, even for a small clinic, were hard to find. The Santi's old church in the Via Cimbri was conveniently sited, largely undamaged, and had a couple of available rooms on the ground floor opposite the chapel. The windows of these rooms were painted white, with a red cross in the centre and the Ecumenical Medical Committee began its first project.

The red cross still remains on the same windows. A table for minor operations rests in the centre of one of the rooms and the clinic continues to offer its service, without cost, to the poor people of the district. In one of the rooms is a filing cabinet, its cards giving the details of each patient. The first card is dated 3rd March, 1946. It is in the handwriting of an American woman, the first of a long series of voluntary assistants. The second is in the writing of Teofilo Santi. From the very beginning of the clinic he was there each day, diagnosing, operating, offering skilled help to the stricken folk of Naples. At the same time he gave spiritual comfort and hope to many who wondered if the struggle to live was truly worth while.

It was when he was at work in the surgery that the crisp-speaking, tidily-groomed American came to visit him.

'Dr Santi?' Teofilo nodded. 'My name is Kellerman, and I'm glad to meet you. Dr Severinghaus told me to look you up when we got to Naples.'

'Let me finish this case and I'll be free to talk.'

Kellerman watched Teofilo dealing with his patient and went on talking. 'He said you were interested in helping the poor ... told me about your family's work at Casa Materna and your own responsibility in the camps.' Teofilo began to write up the case-card. 'Do you have much free time, Dr Santi?'

'None at all. I've got more than enough to do as it is.' Teofilo did not even look up.

'That's a pity. I wanted you to come with me and see how some of the people of Naples are living.'

'I *know* how our Neapolitans are living, Dr Kellerman.' His voice was hard. 'After all they've suffered I'm surprised that some of them are living at all.'

The visitor was not rebuffed. 'You've been to the caves?'

'The caves?' Teofilo dismissed his patient with a handshake and a swift smile. 'No, doctor. I haven't. I'm too busy doing what must be done here to take time off to go and look at them. But, I can imagine what they're like.'

Kellerman's face was strained. 'No one can imagine what they're like. I thought I knew most of the depths of human misery, but when I saw the caves. . . .' He broke off, unable to continue. Then, grasping Teofilo's arm, he pressed him again. 'Come with me. Come and look at them, and tell me what to do.'

It was on the Sunday afternoon that Teofilo went with the American doctor. Unable to believe that things were quite as bad as he had been told, he found that no words could ever have described what he found. The 'caves' of Capodimonte and Fuorigrotta were natural labyrinthine passages in the limestone cliffs and hills above the city, opened out by quarrying, and it was here that the close-packed population of Naples had fled when the air-raids first began. Returning home to the crowded slums they found their houses damaged or destroyed. Left with nowhere to shelter, little groups of homeless people made their way back to the caves with what they could salvage of their possessions. The air-raids grew more regular, more intensive, and more people took to the caves until, in order to escape the bombs or because the poorer quarters of the cities were almost completely destroyed, it seemed that half the population of the slums had sought refuge there. Now, three years after the war was over but with little rebuilding being done, the Neapolitan refugees were still there.

They parked the car and Kellerman led Teofilo into the mouth of one of the 'caves'. Ragged children raced towards them, dirty hands thrust out for alms. Men and women, equally ragged, sat listlessly near the entrance, their faces sullen, their eyes suspicious. They looked sick, hungry and despairing. Kellerman led the way forward and waited until their eyes had grown accustomed to the darkness which was lighted here and there by candle-ends or tiny lamps. At first aware only of the dark and the rustling movements that came through it Teofilo suddenly realised that he was breathing an air fouler than anything he had ever known. It was the stench of over-used air, heavy with human breath and disease ... the stench of the unwashed ... of urine and excrement.

'Some of these caves run for miles' said Kellerman. 'This one is more than three miles long—and the way we have come in is the only exit.'

The nausea in Teofilo's stomach fought its way upwards, slum doctor though he was, but he forced himself to go on. With an elemental desire for privacy families had erected partitions of beaten-out kerosene tins, rags too broken to use as clothes or cardboard cartons soggy with damp.

'Go as far as you like; you'll find people as far as you can go.' Sensing Teofilo's incredulity he went on. 'No one knows how many hundreds, thousands, of people are living here. Some go out to find work, if they can. The children are sent out to beg. The women and girls give themselves to anyone who is prepared to cohabit with such filth. If you go deeper down you'll find people who haven't seen the sun for months.' He stopped speaking as Teofilo turned back.

'Let's get out,' he said. His eyes now accustomed to the darkness, he had seen more than he could bear.

'They're not *all* bad,' said Kellerman as they lurched into the sunlight. 'But it's hard to keep any sort of standards in the caves. Have you seen enough?'

Teofilo did not answer. He was already talking to some of the women at the entrance, asking questions, picking up a sick child in his arms. Kellerman left him talking and went back to the car. He had done what he had been commissioned to do.

'I've told them I'll come back,' Teofilo commented when he got into the car. For the rest of the drive back to Portici he sat silent, withdrawn into his thoughts.

The children at Casa Materna ... the needy people of Portici ... the camp at Capua ... the daily clinic at the Via Cimbri ... true he was not yet married, but Fabio was becoming involved in local politics, and Papa and Mamma were getting older. He himself was young, only thirty-seven, physically fit enough to throw himself into new tasks. But it was not years that mattered; it was hours and minutes. Were there enough unoccupied hours in any week to let him begin something new?

At nine o'clock on Monday morning Teofilo clambered over the uneven ground of the old quarry and looked round. In the face of the hills was opening after opening, the entrance of each cave cluttered with a mobile group of dark-clothed people. He went a little nearer to the biggest of them and put down his black medical bag. Raucous-voiced children started to run towards him, making shrill comments as he set up a small tent. The women followed them.

'Plenty of people come to look at the caves and promise to help us, but they never come back.'

'What's in your bag?'

'We've no money to pay for medicines.'

Teofilo took the hand of a small child, very gently, and drew him forward. 'That's a nasty sore on your leg.'

The child yielded to him as the doctor began to examine it. 'I fell over. A long time ago. It didn't hurt much then, but it does now.'

'We'll see if we can make it better, shall we?' He opened his bag and took out ointment, dressings, a few instruments and put them on the table.

That Monday morning was the beginning of a ministry of healing which lasted for more than three years. Every day, unless something made it completely impossible, Teofilo made his way to the 'caves' and tried to deal with an ever-growing number of patients. They soon discovered that he was no ordinary doctor, for he offered them hope and faith while he ministered to them. He gave them what no one else had given them as long as they could remember—love. It did not concern them whether he was Protestant or Catholic, but lapsed Catholics or Communists though most of them had become, they had no difficulty in finding a name for him that sprang naturally from their town's history and their faith.

'*Sant' Circo Redivivo.*'

Sant' Circo, the doctor-saint of his own Portici, come to life again.

As the months passed, however, Teofilo realised that he was fighting a losing battle. He might heal a few cases each week and relieve many more, but tuberculosis, pneumonia, bronchitis would go on increasing as long as the cave-dwellers remained. What would happen if there were a real epidemic? If typhoid broke out in the caves, for instance? By the end of the 1940s rebuilding was beginning in Naples, but no one in authority had any ideas about rehousing the Neapolitan refugees. Those in the camps might, with the aid of the World Council of Churches, be resettled in new homes and far-off lands. No one could be expected to do the same for the people of Naples, only a few hundred yards from the ruined slums where they had once lived. Teofilo was at heart, like his brother Fabio, not a welfare-worker but a reformer. He saw the task of the Christian not simply as making life easier for those who must live in a broken world, but as remaking the world itself.

In his own tiny segment of the post-war world his task was clear enough. He could not confine himself to helping the cave-dwellers of Fuorigrotta and Capodimonte. He must see that the caves were closed.

With Fabio's help he began to bring pressure on the Mayor of Naples and the Municipality. The caves must be closed. To a man already facing endless major problems the demand was, at first, merely irritating. What could be done with the people if the caves *were* closed? Teofilo stated the answer plainly. The people must be rehoused. Such an answer only high-lighted the absurdity of the demand to close the caves. There was no housing available. Then, pressed Teofilo, some kind of housing must be built.

The population of Naples was more than a million. For a while the struggle to close the caves was the fight of one man against the million who were too busy, too thoughtless, too poor to care. In time Teofilo gained allies in his campaign, some of them in high places and in the City Council itself. He had endless interviews with those who might help, giving up time he felt he should be spending in tending the sick so that a greater good might be done. He pleaded and argued with the mayor himself, until at last capitulation came.

'Very well, Dr Santi. I can see you're right. We will close the caves.'

'And rehouse the people?'

'Certainly. We can't do much, but we'll do what we can. Build them some *barracche*, anyway.'

'Make new slums, you mean?' commented Teofilo. 'Well, even the *barracche* are better than nothing.' He got up to leave. 'Thank you, *signore*. Thank you on behalf of the people of the caves.' At the door he turned again. 'Thank you for your promise. I shall not let you rest until it is fulfilled.'

14

'Casa Mia'

UNDER unrelenting pressure the Mayor of Naples began to look for some way of carrying out his promise and after years of terrible privation which had loosened the moral foundations of life in thousands of families the suspicious and by now often lawless families were moved about 1950 to three groups of settlements. If they were poor by any other standards, they were at least better than the caves. Of the three *barracche*, one was at the Piazza Nationale behind the station, and the other two in Bagnioli. In time new transfers were made to Granili and the 'haunted' buildings of Caserma Bianchini, while the families who had found a temporary home in the Piazza Nazionale were moved to *barracche* at Ponte della Madalena when the magnificent new Stazione Nazionale was built at a cost which would have rehoused the whole population of Naples. But Italy was not alone in this disparity of expenditure.

The resettlement area already had a reputation as one of the worst parts of the city and the newcomers were soon to increase it. Mental images of 'theft', 'violence', 'crime', or 'poverty' depend on the town or country with which they are associated. Only those who know at first hand the squalid, over-heated, densely-packed slum jungle of Naples can properly visualise such words. Many of the men were out of work, with nothing to do but sleep, lounge, plot or quarrel. Where sexual appetites were more easily satisfied than physical hunger, continence was a rare virtue. Fights that sprung from lust or jealousy were more passionate than any that rose from political causes, though politics produced violence enough. Families did not have apartments: they had—or shared— a room. 50,000 children in Naples have never been to school in their lives—and the illiterate, finding less amusement than others in playing games, copy the violence or the stealthy crime of their elders. Harlotry and pimping, to the hungry, was neither immorality nor pleasure. It had become the only way of earning a living for the family. There might be no work for the men in the factories or the docks, but a prostitute was not likely to be unemployed until venereal disease or some jealous drunk's knife put an end to her usefulness.

'Wanna' a girl, Joe?' The familiar whine, the only English words many small boys knew, were a constant horror or temptation to the soldiers and sailors of Naples. Those who hesitated found themselves being dragged into the squalid *barracche* to copulate with the small pimp's sister amidst the filth of stained blankets and orange-boxes that served for stools and tables. They would be fortunate if they escaped without V.D.; unlikely to find their money still in their pockets.

To the families evacuated from the 'caves' after living for three or four years in semi-darkness without work and without hope there was little incentive to rise above the level of their neighbours, although not all those who lived in the *barracche* sank to the common level of violence and immorality. The desire of the few to maintain some sort of integrity, however, only threw the problem into sharper focus. It would be wonderful to save the whole community; it would almost be a miracle to save a few of those who had ideals for their illiterate children even though they had given up hope for themselves.

Time after time Teofilo returned back to Portici from medical work in the *barracchi* wondering if anything at all could be done. Clearly, if a beginning were made it must be with the children, but the hundreds of *barracchi* children could not be handed over to Fabio and Casa Materna. There was neither room nor money for them; parents would not part with their children; nor would the children settle to any ordered life after the wild and dark liberty of the slums. In the over-crowded lanes of Ponte della Madalena there was no room for such schools or play-centres as had been organised in the camps and it seemed that only a major scheme of rehabilitation undertaken by Government or City Council would be of any use.

He was still pondering the impossible when he visited England in the early 1950s. The East End of London was not exactly paradise, even to Teofilo Santi, but it was vastly better than

Naples. What really kindled his imagination, however, was the place in which he stayed—an Anglican Settlement House in Bethnal Green. It was his first introduction to 'settlements' and, because of this, he saw its relevance all the more clearly. 'Welfare work' for youth in Southern Italy all belonged to the realm of 'charity', sometimes cold, mostly institutional. Characteristically, it involved doing something from outside, or taking children out of their old environment. The Settlement House at Bethnal Green was exciting because it showed that something could be done within the situation itself. Here, in London's East End, the nearest thing he could find to the *barracche* situation, was proof that it worked.

Teofilo went back to Naples with new enthusiasm.

It was held within strict bounds because such a scheme would not only need premises, which were not easily found, but money. He knew of no source he could tap for fresh supplies, except those which already provided income for Casa Materna, and it was pointless to divert funds from Portici, which needed all it could get, towards something which after all might fail. Back home, he was already fully occupied and to these commitments he had added a wife and home of his own. He wondered how he had ever imagined he could make time for something new. The squalor of the *barracche* made him restive whenever he went into them but his London-bred enthusiasm was shrinking into the decent proportions dictated by realism.

The conscience of a committed Christian man, however is an awkward companion. He could not get the people who used to live in the 'caves' out of his mind. Till now, he had organised four clinics for them; offered them some sort of encouragement that these deplorable labyrinths would be closed; pressed and prodded until they were rehoused. Now, in their concrete blockhouses and the tenements made out of a haunted mansion falling into ruins, they were beginning life again without any true idea of how to live. He felt increasingly that God would not leave him alone until he was doing still more.

The flashpoint was reached when he was paying a medical call on a businessman. 'I know you're interested in doing something in the *barracche*, doctor. Would it help if I let you have the top part of a small warehouse? There are half a dozen small rooms there—enough to give perhaps even three or four families a bit better home than they have in the *barracche* or the *caserma*.'

Teofilo did not even need to think. 'It would be wonderful, *signore*.' His mind leapt ahead, the dreams from London's East End tumbling into shape against the Neapolitan background. 'But would you mind if we didn't use it for living-space for families? I'd be happier to make use of it for the children in the neighbourhood. We could have schools, a clinic, a sort of club in the evening. There would need to be welfare workers there, of course, and . . .'

'Wait a minute, doctor Santi.' The businessman looked aghast at his enthusiasm. 'How many children do you think you could get into five or six rooms on top of a storeroom?'

'A hundred . . . a hundred and fifty maybe!'

'You're mad, *signore*.' He laughed, sharply and uncertainly. 'But all the Santis have been mad.' He rose and clasped Teofilo's hand. 'Go ahead, doctor. You can have the rooms.'

No sooner did he commit himself to the scheme than proof of its rightness came to hand. The Santis based the 'madness' of their schemes on a deep, unshakable faith in God. Once they responded to the dream He gave them, He would Himself respond by providing some of the means for making it come true. In this case help came from Congregational Christian Service, the organisation founded in the United States by Dr Elmar Severinghaus, whom he had met and who had introduced Dr Kellerman to him. He was promised substantial financial grants towards the creation of his settlement.

From these tentative beginnings came *Casa Mia*—'my home' to thousands of children.

Outside, Casa Mia looks much as it did when Teofilo Santi took it over—a red-brick, two-storeyed warehouse with a corrugated iron gate barring the passage-way that runs beside it. It is dull and unattractive, a little workaday building on the edge of the slums. As the *barracche* are cleared away (and this is being done fairly rapidly) the building itself will no doubt be pulled down to make room for a block of flats or offices. When this is done even the taxi-drivers may find it hard to point out just where it stood. But many hundreds of children will be able to find their way back, though they will be children no longer, for it was here that life really began for them.

After the merchants finally moved their stores out of the ground-floor rooms and left the whole building to Casa Mia, the lower storey housed three store-rooms, a kitchen and a dining-room. The kitchen was dark and steamy and the dining room unpretentious, with a few forms and long, rough, wooden tables. The sun never reached them, for they led off the passage by the side of the building and this passage itself was bounded on the other side by a high block of buildings. On the first floor the half-dozen rooms were used for an office, a clinic, school-rooms and, more lately, a dormitory for six Casa Materna boys attending technical schools or beginning their apprenticeships.

It is incredible that, into these cramped quarters, between 300 and 500 children came every day for schooling and a meal.

It was never Teofilo's intention to do everything himself and his first helper is still there. Miss Hulda Stettler, a tall, grey-haired American woman with a sense of humour and a training in social work which led her never to take anyone, good or bad, at their face value, came to Casa Mia in 1952. She offered to work there for two years, and it seems doubtful if she will ever easily pull up her roots. Just as Congregational Christian Service, with its regular and generous financial help, made Casa Mia a practical possibility, so the Congregational Church in the United States (now the Church of Christ) gave personal help in Hulda Stettler. Teofilo Santi is its Director, but it is round Hulda that the day-to-day work revolves.

This work has been primarily educational. Indeed, because children of kindergarten age must go to school (in theory, at least, though not in fact for tens of thousands in Naples) it is the running of the kindergarten which gives Casa Mia its legal status and has prevented its being closed down when malicious attacks have been made on it. How can more than 300 children be accommodated in an area that Teofilo's friendly patient imagined would serve perhaps four families? Simply by using ever available space and all the hours of the day. From the *barracche* a hundred and fifty or more little boys and girls in their white smocks, tumble into the passageway and up the stairs. The rooms are all pressed into service. The flat roof above the kitchen and store-rooms is used for games and outdoor activities—sometimes hindered by the hens which stray in from nearby houses. In the afternoon, another set of children, about the same in number, pour in and the morning children go home.

Not all the education is limited to primary subjects. Girls over 11 years old learn such practical subjects as pattern-making, cutting-out and dressmaking to qualify them for the state examinations which they must pass before they can find employment in the clothing shops and factories.

As at Casa Materna, all children have hot milk or coffee to drink and a meal at midday or at night.

The teachers, neat and bright in their blue dresses, are all qualified and mostly young. It says much for the atmosphere of this settlement in the *barracche* that they are prepared to work here when teachers of all kinds are in such short supply throughout the whole country.

Apart from the roof the only playground is the entrance passage, where a dozen small boys may be found kicking the ubiquitous football in hopes of one day finding a place in the star-spangled Italian teams.

To the casual reader all that has been written must seem ordinary enough. To the unprivileged people who have surrounded Casa Mia, without the natural human rights of education, decent homes or sufficient food or work, it still remains a matter of astonishment that men and women, some from Naples and others from overseas, should truly care enough to serve them. The underprivileged are naturally suspicious of those who offer something for nothing. Italy is deficient in social welfare schemes and it was a surprise, therefore, when the priests of one of the slum churches were said to be offering *pasta* to all who came. As it turned out, it was not exactly a free gift. The Church, like the Government and most responsible citizens, recognised the dangers of the Communist faith which was competing so successfully for the labouring classes and the unemployed.

'5 lb of macaroni to every worshipper who comes and hands in his Communist party membership ticket at the altar', offered one group of parish priests.

They were at first delighted by the number of Communists who brought their party tickets and went away with their *pasta* under their arms. Their pleasure changed to a fearful amazement at the hundreds of Communists there appeared to be in the *barracche*, as the queue for macaroni showed little sign of drying up.

It was when one of the workers from Casa Mia was visiting in the concrete huts that she discovered the reason. Calling on the old Party chairman because she had heard he was unwell she found him sitting up, wheezing with bronchitis but writing busily. So were his wife and family. Around them were scattered new Party tickets, free to all who asked for them.

The old man laughed at her horrified look. 'They have no love for us. If they offer a bribe we will take it. They're rich and we are poor. By doing this we feed our people and cheat the Church! Why not?'

The trouble with the macaroni offer, from the *barracche* point of view, was that it had strings attached to it. By contrast, the work at Casa Mia was selfless, dictated only by Christian love. Because it was disinterested, children, and to some degree adults, responded to it readily.

It must not be thought that the Church often resorts to such subterfuges to attract its lost or lapsed members. The work of Dom Mario Borelli amongst the *scugnizzi*, the wild children of the slums, so effectively publicised by Morris West in *Children of the Sun*, bears the same mark of dedication and love as that of Teofilo Santi at Casa Mia. Both these activities underline the essential need of Christian welfare work—that people must be loved for themselves alone, and that any attempt to seduce them from whatever personal values and integrity they hold is bound to fail.

Teofilo sees Casa Mia as the prototype of new and bigger settlement work elsewhere in the city. Every Saturday morning there is a staff meeting of all the workers over which he presides. Reports are made on school-work by the teachers and on 'casework' by the social workers who regularly visit the children's homes in the slums. A voluntary worker prepared to teach in school or even do some specialised job must become a friend of the children's parents and families in their own homes if his work is to succeed. The school is a springboard for leaping into what appears a repellent community. There are reports on Saturday morning from the visiting doctor on the children's health and from Hulda Stettler on the Casa Materna ex-students' progress in adult living and college studies. New projects are discussed and criticised with complete freedom, whether they are initiated by the Director himself or by some young member of the staff. (On an occasion when I sat in on the staff meeting arrangements were being made for taking a party of older boys, who attended evening classes at Casa Mia, to Norway for a summer holiday in conjunction with the Norwegian Y.M.C.A.) But it is not only at the staff meeting on Saturdays that Teofilo is found there. Almost every day of the week, he visits the settlement to discuss problems and progress with Hulda Stettler and other staff members.

Apart from Hulda, another member of the staff has been there for years. This is Dr Maida, a Catholic doctor who has held a clinic at Casa Mia every day from 12.0 to 2.30 as a piece of voluntary service.

Volunteer workers have come from many countries. Swiss, Americans, Dutch and British young people have all found a new sense of purpose amongst these bright-eyed, friendly, responsive children of the sun. One of them was a Dutch girl, Den Haan, who had been working there for some time when news reached Italy of the floods which, in 1953, swept over eastern England and, much more disastrously, through the Netherlands.

The people of Ponte della Madalene were much more accustomed to receiving than to giving, and it was an astonishment to all the staff of Casa Mia when, almost as soon as the news was broadcast, they made a voluntary collection throughout the *barracche* and brought the proceeds to Den Haan. Into her hands they piled the heaps of feather-light currency and crumpled notes.

'How much is here?' she asked.

She could hardly credit the answer. '100,000 lire, *signorina*. It is because we love Casa Mia . . . because we love you.'

100,000 lire! Nearly £60. 180 dollars!

The Dutch girl sent it home to the Foreign Minister with a description of the people who had given it and the poverty in which they lived. It was gratefully acknowledged, and everyone thought that was the end of the story. The following year, however, there was a meeting of European Foreign Ministers in Sicily and with some surprise Teofilo received a very official-looking letter from the Dutch Foreign Office. It stated that the Foreign Minister would be stopping briefly in Naples on his way home and wished to see Casa Mia and the people who so generously helped the Dutch people out of their meagre finances.

Almost immediately there was a phone call from the Prefect of Naples, the highest authority in the city. He, too, had had a similar letter. His voice was vibrant with horrified displeasure.

'It cannot be done, of course.'

'Why not?' asked Teofilo, innocently.

The Prefect's voice rose perceptibly. 'The *barracche* are not what we wish to show to visiting Ministers. Everyone knows we are getting rid of them, but it would give a wrong impression. Besides, the *barracche* are full of Communists. There would be incredible danger. He might even be shot.'

'But the Minister has written to me asking . . .'

Teofilo's protest was pushed aside. 'You must come to the station and prevent it. You can tell him all about it instead.'

'At the station?'

'Er . . . of course not. There will be a place for you at the official luncheon. But he is *not* to go to Ponte della Madalena. That is an order!'

'Your Excellency,' acknowledged Teofilo, and put down the phone. It would be pleasant to lunch at the Prefect's residence, but he wondered how much time he would have to tell the Minister about Casa Mia.

The red carpets were out at the Stazione Centrale and the city's dignitaries, stiff in their uniforms or suave in morning coats, bowed with pleasure as the Minister shook their hands.

'I was expecting to see Dr Teofilo Santi,' said the Minister.

Teofilo was summoned from the back of the morning coats and uniforms. He caught the Prefect's eye and saw him frown. 'I am afraid the Prefect does not wish you to come with me,' explained Teofilo. 'A luncheon has been arranged. I can perhaps tell you about it afterwards.' Teofilo spread his hands. 'One cannot bring Casa Mia to the Prefect's residence, of course . . .'

Already the Minister was speaking to the Prefect. 'You are most kind—but I arranged to stop in Naples for only one reason. To thank the poor people who sent us a gift when my country was suffering. Will you arrange that, please.'

'Most certainly, your Excellency.' The Prefect's tone was smooth but there was a tautness in him which implied that he would rather have pushed the Minister back into the train. 'It will be a very brief visit, of course. I do not propose to come myself.'

A few minutes later a truck-load of *carbinieri* crashed through the crowded streets. The sirens of the police cars cleared the way for the limousine in which the Minister sat with Teofilo as it sped through the slippery back streets. With a screech of brakes the outriders drew up outside Casa Mia and leapt into position, hands on their guns, eyes alert for trouble. Had Teofilo drawn up in his own car no one would have noticed: instead, the officious intrusion of the police was followed at once by a surging crowd from the *barracche*.

'There's been an accident . . . a fight . . . a murder at Casa Mia.' The rumour grew in anticipation as it was flung about. Out of the concrete huts they streamed in scores, pressing in on the outraged police. Nothing could have better suited the purpose of the occasion; the *carbinieri* had drawn the crowds as nothing else could have done. With Teofilo as translator the Minister spoke simply about his people and their gratitude. There was no condescension, no hint of 'you poor people of Naples'. He answered their questions, shook their hot hands. When it was all over he went up the steep flight of stairs to be engulfed by the children on the flat roof.

Outside, the *carbinieri* waited impatiently, chaffed by the crowd and recognising a good many old 'customers' amongst them.

Inside, three quarters of an hour later, the telephone rang. Like gunshots from a carbinieri pistol the voice at the other end cracked against Teofilo's ear. They needed no translation to express their mood.

'If that is the Prefect of Naples I will speak to him myself.' The Minister took the phone from Teofilo. 'My apologies, Prefect. I am still at Casa Mia . . . most interesting . . . a wonderful piece of work. I am so glad I arranged to stay for an hour or so here in Naples . . . Your luncheon party? I am so sorry if I have incommoded you. Please apologise to your guests for me . . . I had asked Dr Santi to show me Casa Mia and I had not realised you would wish to arrange an official luncheon.'

The phone rattled again and then, realising that it was the Minister at the receiving end, became a little more discreet. The Dutchman smiled across the check tablecloth in the little staff-room, and his smile embraced them all gaily.

'Yes, that's right. I am having lunch here at Casa Mia with Dr

Santi and his helpers. I will look forward to meeting you at the station before my train leaves.'

There was a pause before the voice spoke again. It sounded as if the owner was having some difficulty in speaking at all.

The Minister's voice was round and cheerful by contrast. 'I'm sure I shall, Prefect. I'm having what the children have ... potato-soup and spaghetti ... quite excellent!'

Casa Mia and Ponte della Madalena never forgot the Dutch Minister's visit. Nor, perhaps, did the Prefect.

Most of the foreign helpers at Casa Mia have been students. Amongst them, however, was a man of very different standing. Indeed, when Teofilo heard about his probable arrival he spread his arms despairingly as he shared his bewilderment with Hulda Stettler.

'He's been posted to us, it seems. A young man who is a pacifist and refuses to go into the American Armed services. Someone had heard of Casa Mia and he's agreed to come here and do a year's voluntary service instead.'

'Bully for him!'

'But you haven't heard the rest of it. He's an actor. A "movie" actor. His name is Don Murray.'

The name meant nothing to them, though to the film-going public of the United States it was not unfamiliar. They merely wondered if they were in for trouble. Students, doctors, teachers were one thing. Communists and toughs they could deal with easily enough. Film actors belonged to another world.

As soon as they met him they knew they need not have worried. Don Murray was a man of deep conviction. As a pacifist from a country where such an attitude was rare he might have been awkward, angular, a man with a chip on his shoulder. Instead, it was soon clear that his non-violence had its springs in Christian compassion. He gave himself to the children of Ponte della Madalena and they responded with trust and affection. Instead of staying for one year he remained for three, and even then he had to tear himself away to return to his film-work in Hollywood. Between Teofilo and himself there had grown a lasting friendship, born of common respect and nurtured through working together. Wherever Don Murray went the needy people of Italy would have a place in his heart. And in his plans, too. Before he left Naples he made a promise to Teofilo.

'When I take up work again I'll see that the refugee children are helped by what I earn.'

Don's promise was kept to the full. His whole personal profit from his first two films were turned over to Italian refugee work. The first was *Bus Stop*, in which he starred with Marilyn Munroe, and the second a powerful social document, *A Hatful of Rain*. In his contract he had made another stipulation. The premiere should be in Naples and Teofilo's huge family should be invited to attend. So it happened that there crowded into the cinema, alongside film-stars and personalities of the film-world in all their exotic glamour, a thousand children from Casa Materna and the *barracche* surrounding Casa Mia. But the social overtones of a world first-night meant nothing to them. The one thing that mattered was that there on the screen was Don, who had lived and worked and played with them for a whole three years.

With his proceeds from these two films Don Murray bought land in Sardinia and, under Teofilo's guidance, selected ten refugee families from the camp at Capua for settlement there. For a while Murray himself worked with them on the farm, until he was sure that they were going to make good. Now, years later, the 'Don Murray Project' still continues its work in Sardinia and new life has come to scores of people because he held so firmly by von Hugel's conviction that, for the Christian, 'caring matters most'.

This, however, was not the end of Don Murray's place in the Santi story. Some time after Fabio's death, when Emanuele was working with Teofilo as a Director of Casa Materna, the phone rang. It was for Teofilo. He jerked back with astonishment as it crackled out its message.

'This is Don Murray speaking from Hollywood.'

'From *where*?'

'Hollywood! Listen, Teofilo—this is urgent. Can you be in Hollywood next Wednesday? There's a big meeting here and I want you to speak at it. Put everything down, and come. It's important that you be here. . . . No, I know you can't get reservations and you haven't got the money. Don't worry about that. Just say you'll come. You'll be hearing from the American Consul tomorrow. 'Bye!'

When he reported the conversation to Emanuele, Teofilo spoke as if he did not believe it had really happened.

Next day he had no doubt. The American Consul asked him to call at his office on urgent business. He reiterated Don Murray's request and, when Teofilo pointed out that he had no passport, assured him that there was no need to worry about formalities. For a short visit he could be accommodated. 'You can leave on Monday. You'll *have* to if you're going to be there in time. TWA will be in touch with you about the flight.'

Still dazed, he answered the phone again. 'Dr Santi? This is Trans-World Airlines. We have a seat reserved for you for the flight to the United States on Monday. This is exceptionally important. We know you're busy but we can have you back by Friday. Mr Don Murray has asked us to insist on your coming. It's a meeting of the greatest importance, and you *must* be there! We'll look forward to seeing you at the airport on Monday.'

Completely nonplussed, Teofilo tried to make sense of the business. Obviously it was something to do with Casa Materna. But how could he fly off across the Atlantic on such an astonishingly vague commission? How, on the other hand, could he refuse if the Consul and the airline were backing up Don Murray's request? In a state of indecision to which he was completely unaccustomed he heard Emanuele pressing him to go. Finally, he rang back to the airline and accepted. Still unsure, he put the receiver back on the hook and wondered what he had let himself in for.

Then, for the first time, a personal tragedy broke into the lives of the children of Casa Materna. On the Saturday when the boys were playing in the concrete yard behind the villa a ball bounced over the wall. A small boy shinned up to the top of the wall and dropped on to the railway line that ran between the house and the beach to retrieve it. With the wall between them none of the children saw what happened. There was the roar of an electric train, a screech of brakes as it shuddered to a stop. Terror-stricken, the children waited for the small boy to come back.

Soon afterwards Teofilo and Emanuele were talking to the railway officials and the police in the big office that looked across the railway line to the bay. There had been no chance to do anything. The boy had been killed instantly, of course. But there would have to be an inquest, and a great many enquiries to be made first, especially amongst the children who had been playing in the yard.

'Hollywood is off.' Teofilo felt too sick about the tragedy to do more than explain perfunctorily to the airways official and the Consul. He still could not understand their insistence that he should go, that he could be back in four days, that he could surely leave everything to his brother. No meeting could be as important as that. Emanuele knew enough to cope with the police, but he was an American citizen and that might make for difficulties. In any case, the children were stricken and he dared not leave them.

He put Hollywood and Don Murray out of his mind.

The police gave no trouble. The inquest was a simple and formal affair. Months later it was agreed that the tragedy had been an accident. Long before that Casa Materna had returned to its normal life.

On the Wednesday evening, when Teofilo Santi should have been in Hollywood, a crowd of people gathered in the television studios. The arc-lights glared and the producers fussed to and fro as the clock ticked on. The announcer stepped forward, smiling but unhappy.

'Unfortunately our guest cannot be with us. There has been an accident in Naples and he has had to stay behind to sort things out. We shall have to make do without him—and there are plenty of people here who can tell his story for him. People who have shared in his work, like Don Murray . . . who owe everything they are to him, like some of our friends from Italy who have settled here in the United States. All the same, it's a great disappointment that the chief actor in it all cannot be here . . .

'Doctor Teofilo Santi of Naples, Italy—*This Is Your Life!*'

While the nation-wide coverage of the famous programme flashed on millions of television screens throughout America, Teofilo paused for a few moments in his work amongst the children to wonder what was really happening at Don Murray's important meeting in Hollywood. Without worrying any further, he gathered the still-saddened children round him, chasing away their sorrows with a smile.

It is not surprising that Teofilo Santi was chosen as a suitable subject for *This Is Your Life*. Even without the project dealt with in the next chapter he has contributed immeasurably to the welfare of thousands of children through the work of Casa Materna and Casa Mia. It is important to note, however, that these two pieces of Christian work are completely different in character and purpose.

Casa Materna is a Home; Casa Mia a settlement. In Casa Materna children live for years within the family, gaining a new security, a sound education and usually a religious basis for life which they will not easily lose. In Casa Mia none of these things are so easy. Children come and go. Nominal Catholics or prospective Communists, they are unlikely to achieve a permanent religious faith as a result of their contact with the settlement.

What then *do* they gain from an experiment which has drawn on the financial, physical and spiritual resources of many people? The answer is simple. They achieve new values. Disinterested service and outpoured love are no more wasted here than anywhere else, and in this moral desert of the *barracche* they have produced a finer harvest than anyone who knew the district might imagine to be possible. More important than the education which has fitted many boys and girls to take jobs they could otherwise never have considered, or the food and physical health which have been part of Casa Mia's service to the community, the standards and values of Christian people from many countries have resulted in a new faith and a new idealism. Casa Mia is an experiment which has fully justified everything which has been put into it.

15

Operation Ecumene

'CAN you come and have coffee this evening?'

Teofilo's reply was a little impatient, for it was the second time his friend had made the same request. 'I'm sorry. No. I told you before.'

'It could really be important to you. Dr Chandler is anxious to meet you.'

'Who is this man?'

'He's the Secretary of the Congregational Union of the United States.'

'I'll try and make time to meet him tomorrow. My surgery is full and I've some patients to see afterwards.'

The caller, one of the organising secretaries of relief work in Naples, was growing impatient, too. 'Tomorrow is no use. He's flying back to the States tonight.'

Teofilo sighed, and looked at his visiting-list again. 'All right. I'll try. But remember, I can't promise.'

'You know he wants to talk about the hospital?'

The phone clicked and went dead. Teofilo replaced the receiver and leaned back in his chair, wiping the perspiration away from his eyes. The hospital ... the most evanescent of all the Santi dreams ... the vision his father, Riccardo, had cherished from his first arrival in Naples ... the project which Fabio created again in vivid phrases ... the hospital. ... Teofilo ran his fingers through his dark curly hair and went to the window. It still remained impossible.

The impracticable dream had first been suggested as early as 1895, even before Riccardo Santi had left his theological college in Rome. A hospital run by the Protestant Church, perhaps no more than a few beds for the sick. But for a tiny, dispirited community the idea was absurd. Riccardo raised it again in 1904, after he had settled in Naples, but the next year he found himself involved in the slow unplanned making of Casa Materna. The suggestion did not arise again until after the Second World War when the Evangelical Clinic was opened in the Via Cimbri. Shortly afterwards had come Dr Kellerman's visit and the daily clinics at the 'caves'. On the face of it this was as much as the Evangelicals could hope to do. It was Fabio, seemingly driven by his inner conviction of 'so much to do in so little time', who had raised the matter again in the 1940s.

'The caves and the clinics are only nibbling at the problem,' he asserted. 'We have formed a medical committee and we need a hospital. It's no use saying it couldn't be done. Casa Materna couldn't be done—and yet it is here. Where's your faith, Teofilo?'

Teofilo, never a cautious man, shook his head. 'You're going too fast. We've more than we can cope with now, Fabio. We'd need money. Thousands of dollars. And land. Do you think the municipality would ever give planning permission for a *Protestant* hospital, man? They wouldn't even allow us to buy the ground for it!'

Fabio waved his wide, spatulate fingers across the bay. 'That's where it should be—where everyone can see it—on Posillipo!' His look was that of a man who never tired of fighting for the impossible. 'You find the money, Teofilo. I'll find the land.' But, with his impulsive person out of the room, the temperature dropped again. It couldn't be done.

Now, five years later, Teofilo dismissed his last patient and scanned down his visiting-list. With luck, if nobody kept him too long, he might just manage that cup of coffee, after all.

He made it, with minutes to spare, and the Neapolitan host made the introductions. 'Dr Edgar Chandler ... Dr Santi.' He spoke briskly. 'Dr Chandler knows about Casa Materna ... Capua ... the caves ... but it's the hospital that interests him.'

'How long have you got?'

Chandler looked at his watch. 'I'm due at the Naples airport in half-an-hour.' His voice, thought Teofilo, had the same magnetism as Fabio's. 'Have you got a car?'

'Yes.'

'O.K. You can drive me to the airport. But you'll have to get the whole story into thirty minutes.'

Between these two men there was an immediate rapprochement. Teofilo, his work limited to Naples, was unconfined in vision. Edgar Chandler was soon to become the controller and inspiration of the World Council of Churches Inter-Church Aid and Refugee Services. As the old Fiat clattered along the road to the airport, snatching at every gap in the traffic, Teofilo used his right hand to expound the dream, his stubby forefinger to drive home his points.

This should be an Evangelical Hospital, yes; but it must also be completely ecumenical . . . no, it was not the product any anti-Roman feeling; only a response to need . . . of course there might be opposition, probably there would be on the City Council, but Evangelical-Catholic relationships were simpler than they used to be . . . there was more personal understanding, at any rate . . . he had no proper idea of what it would cost . . . infinitely more than the Evangelicals of Naples could raise . . . it must include a surgical block . . . probably the emphasis should be on geriatrics; old people were largely uncared for everywhere . . . how many beds? As many as they could manage . . . yes, Fabio had had his eye on a site on Posillipo for some time, but whether they could ever get it. . . . Teofilo shrugged his shoulders as the car rushed into the airport, and he braked sharply and leapt out to help Edgar Chandler with his baggage. The flight was already being called.

'You'll be hearing from me, Dr Santi.' As he spoke Dr Chandler was gone.

A month later a letter arrived from the United States. Teofilo read it and then thrust it across the table to his brother. Even Fabio gaped.

'This is the green light, Teofilo. God has told us to go ahead.'

The Congregational Christian Union offered 30,000 dollars towards the cost of the Hospital! The Hospital Committee met and thanked God for his goodness. Two years later it seemed that their prayers of thanksgiving in the committee had been foolishly premature.

Through an intermediary a site was purchased without much difficulty on the crest of the Posillipo ridge, with a view that swept across the whole of the bay to Vesuvius, Sorrento and Capri, one of the most magnificent positions in the whole of Naples. To add to its charm were three cypress trees, the only ones of their kind on the ridge. Admiring them, the Hospital Committee had no idea how much trouble they were to cause.

Foundations were laid, a service of dedication held, and the first outline of the buildings began to rise on the hill-top. Then, with less warning than an eruption, came a letter from the Mayor of Naples. The building was to be halted immediately, and under no circumstances was it to be continued. The mayor's ostensible objections were double-barrelled. The hospital, dominating Posillipo, would destroy the best panoramic view in Naples and change the character of the district. It would also spoil the Neapolitan's view of some of his most cherished treasures, the three cypress trees.

A long and tedious legal battle began, but its outcome was never in doubt. The Neapolitans did not want their precious cypress trees lost. More important, the mayor was determined not to have a Protestant hospital. He insisted that Naples was a Catholic city. He eventually died in a night-club but he saved his city from the ignominy of the hospital. Or so it seemed to him. It caused him no concern that he had left the Evangelicals with a costly site on their hands and no money to spend on a less desirable location somewhere else.

Teofilo looked into the future without hope. He himself had spent many hours in discussion with the mayor, uselessly trying to persuade him to change his mind. Fabio had used his legal skill to circumvent the authoritarian decision, entirely without success. The site was lost. What was worse, the money so generously donated by Dr Chandler and the American churches was lost, too.

Then the miracle happened.

Once more, it was heralded by an unlikely angel with an American accent. A United States Army sergeant arrived at Casa Materna with a message. 'Admiral Kearney would like to see Dr Teofilo Santi.' By the 1950s N.A.T.O. was establishing itself in Naples and the American admiral was the Commander-in-Chief of N.A.T.O. forces in the Mediterranean. The N.C.O. had no idea what the admiral wished to talk about but the Americans were closely interested in the affairs of Casa Materna, and more than one high ranking officer had lately been of great help. It was a surprise when the admiral opened the conversation with naval forthrightness.

'The United States families attached to N.A.T.O. are in need of an American school, Dr Santi, and we want to build it quickly. Our personnel is increasing very rapidly.' The N.A.T.O. headquarters, where he was sitting, were on the wealthy slopes of Posillipo. So were the family quarters. 'We need a site. At once. We understand you have some land that you can't use. It's exactly where we want to put the school, and we'll buy it from you.'

The 'top brass' of the American services did not easily take 'no' for an answer. Still less did the high officers of N.A.T.O. Teofilo put the difficulties succintly but honestly. He explained about the hospital project, and was frank in his opinion that the City Council was not likely to allow anyone else to spoil the panoramic view of Posillipo. After all, he explained, there were the only three cypress trees in Naples to be preserved.

'If N.A.T.O. wants the site I think we'll be able to get it.' The admiral was brusque. 'That's our worry. Yours is the hospital. I see your position, doctor. If the City Council is able to help *us*—and I have no doubt they will!—I think we may be able to help *you* at the same time!'

Teofilo drove home exuberantly to report to Fabio and Papa.

N.A.T.O. not unnaturally got what it wanted, permission to build a school for American children. By 1953 the Sherman Forrest School was in use. At the same time it entered into an astonishingly generous agreement with the Hospital Committee. The United States was to have full use of the premises for nine years. After that, it would pay the Evangelical Hospital Committee a rent of 9,000 dollars a year.

If they could find another site convenient for their purpose the hospital could, once more, become a practical idea. From 1962 there would be a guaranteed income and, if the Americans ever released their tenancy of the Sherman Forrest School, the value of land on Posillipo would have risen to undreamt of heights. It had cost 15,000 dollars. What it would fetch was unpredictable. The Committee met to consider the future.

No group could have been representative of the Evangelical life of Naples. Waldensians, Methodists, Congregationalists, Baptists, the Salvation Army, the Pentecostals and the Seventh Day Adventists were all members of the Committee. At the 'working level' it was wider still. In the clinics, by this time supported by the Committee, seven doctors were at work. Two of them were old students of Casa Materna. Two others were Roman Catholics. In face of human need the traditional barriers of religious life were beginning to break down, as they were already doing in the community life of Portici.

To the Hospital Committee it was already evident that the choice of their original site might, in the long run, have been the wrong one. True it had a wonderful view and would be visible for miles. But it was also becoming more and more the home of the rich, the socially-minded and the N.A.T.O. officers and staff. Would the poor of Naples readily make their way into such an area? Would they, indeed, be prepared to climb a hill to a hospital if they were sick? Now they thanked God for the delays which had prevented their going forward. The lesson of Casa Mia was patent. If you truly want to help people you must be in their midst, not come in from outside or expect them to come to you. The ultimate aim must be not merely to heal human bodies but to transform the lives of people. Already both Teofilo and Fabio were beginning to dream of more extensive service than a hospital. But where should it be?

'This is Vitolo.' The phone call, a year or so later, was from an old friend, an architect. 'I think I've come across a site that might interest you for the hospital.'

'Where?'

'In Ponticelli. A big area. Nine acres. There's some farm land and fruit trees. The only trouble is that there'd be a lot of negotiation to be done. More than one owner, you know. A sort of roadway down the side of the fields and all sorts of people probably have rights to it. Anyway, go and see it. Tell me what you think.'

Ponticelli! What Teofilo thought about that area could be expressed very briefly, even without seeing the site. It was one of the most notorious districts of Naples, worse even than the *barracche* of Ponte della Madalena. Nothing could be imagined at a greater extreme from the original site on Posillipo. Did that mean it was good or bad? The old Fiat rattled out of Portici and nosed its way on an exploration of Ponticelli.

The problems endemic to all the poorer parts of Naples were found here at their most acute. Not far from the industrial belt of the city, unemployment was nevertheless the most deplorable feature of life. Boys grew into manhood without work, and some of their fathers had been unemployed for years. It was not surprising that most of the population was militantly Communist, with no faith in Government or Church. For the youth of the place there was nothing to do but lounge in the shabby *piazza* or, when any money was available, spend the evening lazing in the cafés and bars. Prostitution and crime were part of the normal way of life. Washing hung listlessly across the streets. Animals fouled the courts. Children were everywhere, of every age, in every state of dress and undress—and for the thousands of children in Ponticelli there was only one school.

As Teofilo drove through the thronged passages that served as streets, slippery with filth, there were many who stared at his neat person and shrewd eyes, assessing what he might want. Every glance he met was suspicious, the slackly hanging arms and loose fists all hostile. Turning back outside the town to look at the site Vitolo had found, a great unease swept through him. This was not like the caves or the *barracche*. Here he had no friends. The barriers between the dispossessed and those who came to serve them would not easily be broken down.

He stopped the car at the entrance to the fields. Beyond them were the jagged roofs of Ponticelli. At one side was a rutted pathway with houses backing on to it. He got out of the car and picked his way through the mud and cart-tracks. There were no answering smiles to his own friendly words. The farmer, bending over a hoe, did not even look up from his work.

The ground bore a thin crop, and was so extensive that even a biggish hospital would not use half of the space. The farmer would still be able to carry on his work even if it were built. Yes . . . yes, he thought to himself, this could well be the place for it. But would the farmer and those who had rights here ever sell to a stranger, to the Church and a Protestant Church at that. How long it might take to come to some agreement it was impossible to say. But . . . he looked at the uneven tenements . . . the sharp voices of the children came back at him from the houses beside the field . . . the farmer unbent his back slowly and stared at him across the handle of the hoe . . . yes, thought Teofilo, this is the place if we can get it. Here we shall be at the hub of a great circle of human need.

OPERATION ECUMENE

A year later the architect, Vitolo, gave him the answer he feared. So many people who owned rights to the pathway refused to negotiate that it seemed hopeless to continue. The farmer himself would be happy enough about the deal but the Communists would not allow any Church to gain new concessions. Two Catholic priests with rights to the field path refused to sell.

'If Fabio had been here . . .' began Vitolo. Teofilo visualised Vitolo's fatalistic gesture. But Fabio had been killed soon after the Americans had taken the Posillipo site. Without his brother's ebullient enthusiasm to keep hope alive Teofilo made a flat reply.

'It's no use, Vitolo. I thought we'd never get it!'

Slowly at first, then with an aching desire to forget the tragedies that had hammered away at the foundations of the family's life, Teofilo drove himself back to work at Casa Materna, at Casa Mia, amongst his patients. The mood of despair passed as Emanuele took a heavier part of the load at Casa Materna. It was a pity to give up the hospital project, but the disappointment was lessened by the accomplishments at Casa Materna. At Casa Mia, the results were less spectacular but no less real. Not least was there hope in the new religious climate. In Rome, 'Good Pope John' was holding gentle hands of friendship to other communions. The 'heretics' of Papa Santi's early days in Naples and Portici were newly loved and prayed for as 'separated brethren'. The trust and affection between divided congregations in Portici were seen to have an unsuspected Papal blessing, to have anticipated the mood of those who declared the will and nature of God.

Other demands were made on Teofilo. Fabio had been a member of the city council; why should he not follow in his brother's way? His medical colleagues, devout or agnostic, urged him to put his almost unique knowledge at the service of the town. In the late 1950s he accepted their pressure and stood as a candidate for the Portici Council. From the time his name was announced there was no doubt that he would be elected. Within three years he had followed Fabio into the deputy-mayor's chair. His hands strayed over the plans for a public hospital for Portici . . . Fabio's plans . . . and he began the pressure which was to lead to their fulfilment. The Santis were still building for the future.

In 1963 the world was saddened and Italy itself stricken by the death of Pope John XXIII. Portici went into mourning and

Evangelicals shared the Catholics' sadness of the loss of one who had done so much to bring a new vision to the Church. The Portici City Council prepared for a public oration on his life and work. 'There is only one man fitted to make such a tribute.' The judgment of the Council was unanimous and spontaneous. Teofilo Santi, Methodist lay preacher, delivered a deeply sincere oration, widely reported in the press, an Evangelical's tribute to one of the world's greatest figures, whose heart had been stirred by the same compassion for the poor as his own.

A year after the first set-back in the hospital's affairs at Ponticelli, the architect Vitolo phoned once more. 'Can you come to my office as soon as possible? I've got some good news for you.'

In the office he went into fuller detail. 'The sale of the Ponticelli land has been agreed. There are twenty-nine different landowners who have rights over the roadway, and they're all willing to sign agreements.'

'What about the two priests?'

'In the presbytery another priest urged that the land be sold. You know the Gamaliel story in the Acts ... "If this thing be of God we cannot fight against it, if it be of man it will come to naught!" I gather he took the same line. He knew of you through Casa Mia.'

The agreements were signed, plans drawn up, tenders scrutinised. With the rent of the Forrest Sherman School available from 1962, after the Americans nine-year tenancy, and with other funds from overseas, the first stage was in sight. The contractor, a friendly builder named Cerini, cut down costs so sharply that it seemed unlikely he would even meet his expenses, far less make any worthwhile profit. From Geneva came the assurance that the World Council of Churches, of whose social welfare committees Teofilo was a member, was deeply interested in the scheme. The cost sounded enormous—140 million lire for the first part of the scheme. £80,000 or 250,000 dollars. The only thing was to go forward in faith.

This is precisely what the Hospital Committee has been doing ever since. There are many problems still to be faced. Only two floors of the hospital can be attempted for the time being. An ecumenical labour camp staffed by young people of many countries had to be given up because the Communists would have fomented trouble by insisting that the foreigners were taking employment and money from local workers. Staffing will not be easy. Nurses, like all vocational workers in Italy, are in short supply and it may be necessary to seek for skilled help from VSOs or perhaps nursing deaconesses from other countries in Europe, though some Casa Materna girls are already in training outside Italy. The architect's drawing provides for an outer shell; the building must be furnished with everything from operating-table and sterilisers to sheets and bedpans.

On the other hand, the problems are outweighed by practical help promised and, more particularly, by the spectacular achievement of a new Evangelical unity. Churches have promised items of equipment. Individuals and organisations will make their own contributions. If nursing staff is hard to come by, medical staff is already interested. With the Waldensian, Colonel Paulo Nitti, as vice-chairman of the Committee and Teofilo Santi as Director, despite their heavy commitments elsewhere, the outreach into a sympathetic medical profession is already considerable. Catholics and Evangelicals will work side by side in the wards and in the operating theatres. The faith of the Santis knows no limits. They respond to need, knowing that in doing so they are responding to God Himself.

One afternoon, while the first part of the hospital was still under construction, I went with Teofilo Santi to see it, surrounded by wooden scaffolding. Contractor Cerini, with a roll of plans in his hand, waited to welcome us by the builder's hut. Inside, on the wooden table covered with detailed drawings, stood a straw-covered bottle of chianti and some sticky iced cakes in a paper bag. The foreman and sub-foremen crowded in, all talking at once, to share the occasion even though it was a Saturday afternoon. They explained the plans, offered drawings of the hospital with one hand and sun-warmed chianti with the other. Outside, workmen —bricklayers, cement-mixers, barrow-pushers—talked volubly to Teofilo. To the contractor and workmen, as well as the Director, this was *their* hospital.

Down the path, his spare form graced by his best suit, the farmer waved and waited. His straw hat left on the peg, he doffed his felt one and thrust his hard hand into ours. 'You must come to our house.' There was no time for refusal; we were already grasped, one by each arm, and piloted down the path which twenty-nine separate owners had handed over to the hospital. The house was spotless and charming, the furniture very modern, a light veneered walnut. The wife almost curtsied us inside, and the young son and daughter-in-law laid biscuits and vermouth on the table. The talk twisted from health to the field crops, from their holiday at the sea-side to the progress of the building. It was a long time later that we left, for Teofilo, with endless tasks unfinished and some not yet begun, always has time to talk to his friends.

That was the secret of our hospitality. These people were friends. Like the contractor and his workmen, the gap was bridged already by a true interest in all they did. Ponticelli is still the wild place it was, its rebels untamed, its children illiterate, its narrow streets and shabby squares dull or frightening. But there, too, without doubt, once the hospital is built, the wide divisions of religion, culture and politics will have bridges built across them.

From the contractor and the farmer we made our way back to the shell that was soon to be a hospital, climbing up ricketty wooden ladders to the fresh concrete that was already hardening into the first floor. Beyond the farmland, still tilled by the old man, stood the homes of Ponticelli. Behind us ran the making of a new road, for the hospital will stand at the side of a great new autostrada leading from Sicily to Rome.

Teofilo pointed out the kitchens, the sterilising room, the operating theatres, the wards, so far no more than squares of unfaced brick. He waved his arm above our heads, where eventually there would be two more storeys. 'When we shall build them I can't say. It depends on so many things. The Evangelical churches are not strong or wealthy. We have to go on relying on help from overseas. I hope it will be done while I'm here.' He looked suddenly serious, this short, stocky man in a thick overcoat, hands thrust into his pockets. Optimism and strength radiated from him and, like his friendship, sparked to a flame the same spirit in those who knew him. 'I'm not so young as I was. Fifty-five this year. But I'd like to see it finished.'

'How many beds will there be?' I asked. It was not a moment for light banter. Papa had lasted until he was almost ninety but in these days all men live under stress.

'Sixty to begin with, I hope. It will be geriatric, for the most part. The old have too little attention in Italy. It will be good to care for them here.' His eyes lit with enthusiasm as he clasped my arm. 'But the main thing about it is that it is an *ecumenical* hospital. That's the great point. The Evangelical churches have been for so long introspective and pietistic, frightened to move out in case they moved too far for their own safety. Now, in this, they are reaching out—and doing it together. This is wonderful. This is a work of God.' His glance swept the unfinished building. 'It will be opened in 1966—the first Ecumenical Hospital in Europe.'

We stood silent, meditating on a miracle. For me, these days in Naples since Teofilo had met me at the Stazione Centrale had been an unfolding story of miracle after miracle. I thought of Riccardo Santi, taking two little children home because he had heard God's voice, and of all that had come from that act of faith. I thought of Teofilo and Fabio breaking down the high barriers by personal service, of all they had given to the Church and the community. I thought of Emanuele, too busy now to touch his beloved violin, surrounded by children in Casa Materna. I remembered Capua, the 'caves' and Casa Mia. Amongst the scaffolding of the unfinished building I knew that in the Santi story I had come upon one of the most wonderful stories of our time.

Teofilo was speaking again, his firm hand gripping my arm. He raised his other hand and pointed to the farmland between ourselves and Ponticelli.

'Do you know what I want to see there on that ground, dear friend?' His voice gathered new strength. 'A nurses' home, of course. That we *must* have. But I want more than that. I think there must be a home . . . two homes . . . for old people. One for those who are single. Another for retired pastors of the Evangelical churches and their wives. Here they would learn to go on living. Think of what it could mean to Ponticelli, to Naples!

'And I want to plan for a students' house, for ex-pupils of Casa Materna. Like those six boys at Casa Mia. Somewhere for them to live together and study for their apprenticeships, where they can bring the security of Casa Materna and yet learn to live in the world.

'Casa Mia! Yes, the days of Casa Mia are numbered in Ponte della Madalena as the *barracche* are being swept away. But here in Ponticelli, where the children do not go to school and the young people only have the bars at night—what could not a New Casa Mia do here!'

He fell silent again. His dreams seemed so remote from present reality . . . created out of the fragile stuff of impossibilities. Yet had not every part of the Santi story been fashioned by faith from the same fabric?

As we picked our way to the rickety ladder and down to the ground I knew that the Santi story was far from finished yet.

Postscript

SINCE this book was first published seven years ago it has been translated into Swedish, German and Dutch. Emanuele has travelled scores of thousands of miles, playing his 'Strad' and telling the story of the years. Every year more people hear, read or see for themselves the miracle of love that the Santi family have created and sustained for three quarters of a century.

New friends are made, and their support is needed as much as ever.

But new friends, and older ones, ask questions.

What has happened in the last decade? How do these institutions fit into the pattern of a changing Italy, where social structures alter and pressure is put on government to accept its own responsibilities for those in need? What is the future likely to be?

In a very brief postscript let me give some indications of answers.

In terms of service and compassion there are no real changes. Love, resulting in service without any strings attached, is the code determining all that the Santis do. In terms of quality, Casa Materna has constantly to meet new standards set down by government departments. Yet a government inspection in 1970/71 had little but praise for all they saw. There have been improvements. New sewage disposal tanks have been installed below sea level, for instance, and excellent new school furniture has been fitted. There is a constant attention to small, detailed amenities. The children look better dressed, and more informally so ... often in clothes which proclaim their American origin.

Yet, in the main, Casa Materna must still depend on personal and private support. Rigid resistance to any sort of state support, which would involve a measure of state control, is maintained. More private subscribers and fresh donors would mean new ability to meet rising costs and provide more up-to-date facilities.

To the visitor from Britain or America the conditions in the dormitories, for instance, look spartan and overcrowded—until one sees how other Italian 'homes' and 'orphanages' are maintained. What makes Casa Materna infinitely more acceptable than most is the quality of love that pervades it.

No children in Italy are happier, more relaxed and secure, than these children.

Yet it is an island in a national sea whose waves begin to beat more rigorously.

There is more state care than previously. State security benefits and a national health service have greatly altered the situation within the last twenty years or so. The day of the private institution, however excellent, will not last for ever. It is clear that, if Casa Materna is to survive—and that it ought to do so as a non-state institution is beyond question—changes must come, and quickly. A much closer link with the Church—and, indeed, as in the case of the Ecumenical Hospital, with all the Churches—is essential. It is hoped that a strong ecumenical committee may come into being with fuller support from within, as well as outside of, Italy. A new note of confidence must be given to the organisation, and this can only be from a broader-based constitution.

Children now come for shorter periods, often sent by the local municipality. There are fewer orphans than there were. Broken or disrupted families provide most of the intake. Closer links with children's own homes are desirable, and it would be good to have qualified social workers as members of the staff. International voluntary workers have provided a steady stream of support during the past few years but there remains a dearth of qualified, long-term workers from Italy itself. In all organisations this is a permanent and acute problem.

The school grows in numbers and popularity. There are still very few schools where full-time (that is, all-day) education is offered. Its academic standard is higher than most. At the same time, because of increased opportunities for apprenticeships, and industrial growth in the north, there are now few boys in the carpenter's shop and the machine-shop. They served an excellent purpose, but there is less need of them than there was.

In contrast with Casa Materna, only now beginning to come to terms with a changing world, the sudden and splendid growth of the Evangelical Hospital, very much part of the modern scene, underlines what can be done with a wide committee and even wider contacts.

Dr. Teofilo Santi has become a European figure of considerable stature. He was a pioneer of KEK, the Conference of European Churches, which includes both western and eastern Europe, and is one of its Presidents. There is more in this than honour. He was, for instance, one of a small group which went to Russia to interview the heads of state in an attempt to win fuller freedom for depressed religious minorities. A film of his life and work was made a couple of years ago for the Dutch television service and attracted a great deal of interest and support. This wide publicity and recognition stems very largely from the creation of the Evangelical Hospital.

What was once no more than a dream in the minds of Teofilo and Fabio Santi is now a solid building of concrete and marble, in itself a miracle of compassion as remarkable as Casa Materna was in its early years.

Standing in Ponticelli, that still rather squalid Communist suburb of Naples, it faces the new *autostrada* which runs from Milan to Sicily. At first sight the most outstanding features are the extraordinarily modern buildings. Excellent halls, consulting-rooms, laboratories; small wards, with no more than three patients in each; splendid operating theatres. At closer inspection, the focus changes. What is impressive are the results—operative successes; advances in techniques; pioneering papers submitted by the staff to learned medical journals.

Yet the real marvel here is the sense of fellowship and integration which makes possible the outstanding professionalism of the hospital. The committee includes all the main Protestant denominations in Italy. The nursing and administrative staff are not only as fully ecumenical but also remarkably international. German nursing deaconesses have been matrons from the opening of the hospital. There are Italians, Americans, British and others to be found on the staff. The most startling list is that of the medical and surgical consultants. Fourteen or more range from Roman Catholic to Pentecostal. Half are members of the Medical School of the Naples University. Their service is voluntary.

Patients pay if they can—but some, like an old Yugoslavian refugee woman from the camps, are assured of skilled care and understanding love if they have nothing at all.

As soon as the hospital is fully paid for—and this day is coming much quicker than anyone believed possible—the next stages, already on the drawing board, will begin. More and better nurses' quarters . . . a new 'Casa Mia' to replace the social centre now being run in the shadow of the hospital . . . a home for the elderly, and especially for retired evangelical pastors.

These plans are not mere dreams. Dreams come true in the hands of the Santis.

Their dreams have always been based on faith, and fashioned in hard work. Both dreams and hard work are still necessary in modern Italy—and especially in the south, so tragically different from the prosperous north.

Needs change—but the need remains.

C.J.D.
1973